UPLIFT

D0284161

STORIES

UPLIFTING STORIES

TRUE TALES TO INSPIRE YOU TO TAKE ACTION

IONE BUTLER

TILLER PRESS

NEW YORK   LONDON   TORONTO   SYDNEY   NEW DELHI

TILLER PRESS

An Imprint of Simon & Schuster, Inc.
1230 Avenue of the Americas
New York, NY 10020

First Tiller Press trade paperback edition April 2020

TILLER PRESS and colophon are trademarks of Simon & Schuster, Inc.

For information about special discounts for bulk purchases,
please contact Simon & Schuster Special Sales at 1-866-506-1949
or business@simonandschuster.com.

The Simon & Schuster Speakers Bureau can bring authors to your live event.
For more information or to book an event contact the Simon & Schuster Speakers
Bureau at 1-866-248-3049 or visit our website at www.simonspeakers.com.

Interior design by Laura Levatino
Jacket design by Patrick Sullivan
Jacket art by Kevin Benevides

Manufactured in the United States of America

1   3   5   7   9   10   8   6   4   2

Library of Congress Cataloging-in-Publication Data has been applied for.

ISBN 978-1-9821-3823-3
ISBN 978-1-9821-3824-0 (ebook)

For my mum.

Thank you for all you have done for me.

TABLE OF CONTENTS

UPLIFTING
STORIES

INTRODUCTION

Do you sometimes despair at the state of the world? Are you disappointed with the people in it? If so, you are not alone. I'm sure we can all relate to feeling deflated at times, especially after watching the evening news. Most media outlets stream a steady diet of depressing and scandalous stories, because strife and conflict sells. And it's human nature to be drawn to it. In fact, it's in our DNA: what scientists call the "negativity bias" was essential to our survival back in the caveman days, when our ancestors had to be keenly aware of every threat to their safety. But while times have changed, biology hasn't. It's what keeps us devouring the news and in a constant state of stress.

This relentless consumption can be seriously detrimental to our mental health, and even our physical health. Psychologist Graham Davey says, "Negative news can significantly change an individual's mood—especially if there is a tendency in the news broadcasts to emphasize suffering and also the emotional components of the story. In particular, negative news can affect your own personal worries. Viewing negative news means that you're likely to see your own personal worries as more threatening and severe."

In fact, it was this realization, that what we consume has

such a profound effect on us, that led me to create Uplifting Content in 2016—a social media platform, blog, podcast, and now a book with a twofold mission: 1. to uplift humanity by creating and sharing inspiring media, and 2. to empower people to take positive action in their lives.

I started it, in part, for my own benefit, because most of my life I've dealt with depression. When I was feeling low, I'd seek out inspiring movies, TV shows, and online content, but they were surprisingly difficult to find. I also learned some sad and shocking statistics—that nearly 1 in 5 American adults, or 60 million people, suffer from mental health issues. That there are 123 suicides per day in the United States; that's one every 11 minutes. And that for every successful attempt, there are 25 failed attempts.

People are struggling. I've developed strategies over the years to cope with depression, and positive narratives are a huge part of that. I couldn't believe how quickly they improved my mood and emotional well-being, and I was called to gather healing messages and share them with the millions of people who needed to hear them.

Because it's not all doom and gloom. You might be surprised to learn that in the last sixty years, the percentage of the world population living in extreme poverty (surviving on $1.90 a day or less) shrank from 50 percent to 10. Life expectancy rose by twenty years. Global literacy rates have also jumped, from 36 percent in 1950 to 83 percent today. Vastly more people today have rights, conveniences, and protections they never would have dreamed of only twenty years ago. Again, though it might not feel like it, even racism, sexism, and homophobia are on the decline across the board.

If you want to improve your mood, a great place to start is by shifting the narrative. Yes, there are awful people in the world doing horrendous things, but there are also millions upon millions of hardworking parents, friends, citizens, and public servants doing their best to help others. Some of them are the unsung heroes you're about to meet in this book. It's about perspective, paying more attention to things that bring you joy and focusing less on what brings you down.

So here's an experiment for you. Try *not* watching—or reading, or listening to—the news for a week, and see how you feel. I guarantee that the world will not stop spinning because you're no longer tuning in. And when you stop letting all that negativity seep into your subconscious, you'll feel so much better.

And while you're on your news hiatus, enjoy this book. I want to offer you a different lens through which to view the world, and the people in it.

HOW TO USE THIS BOOK

YOU CAN EITHER read it cover to cover or read stories from the relevant chapters to help with whatever you are going through. For example, if you're feeling a little lonely or having a disagreement with a loved one, read the stories from the Human Connection chapter.

If you feel like you'd like to give something back, the Acts of Service stories will inspire you to get started. If you are faced with an overwhelming challenge, the stories from the

Overcoming Adversity chapter will remind you that you can persevere. If you have an idea to challenge the status quo or want to take a stand for what you believe in, the Game-Changers stories are the ones to turn to. If you're feeling stuck in a rut at work, the Pursuing Your Passions and Purpose chapter will get your creative juices flowing. And the stories from the chapter on The Unimaginable will blow your mind when you realize what human beings are truly capable of.

I want these stories to not only lift you up, but also inspire you to take action. At the end of every story, you'll find recommended exercises from either the interviewee or me. They might entail something as simple as smiling at someone on the street or something a bit more difficult, like tackling an issue that matters to you. So grab a notebook, a pen, and a highlighter, take notes, and follow through. I'd love to hear how you get on with the exercises, so please share your success and wins with me on social media @ionebutler.

My hope is that this book and the stories in it remind you of what is achievable. I believe you have unlimited potential. You can make great changes in your life, fulfill your dreams, and make a positive impact on the lives of others and on our planet, if you so desire. Humanity is at a crossroads, and we need you to keep shining your light and sharing your gifts, not to succumb to despair and fear.

So settle in, turn off your phone, and enjoy.

Much love,
Ione

PART 1

HUMAN CONNECTION

Human connection is the most vital aspect of our existence,
without the sweet touch of another being, we are lonely
stars in an empty space waiting to shine gloriously.

Joo Straynga

Abraham Maslow was an American psychologist known for his theory of the hierarchy of human needs, and his famous five-tiered pyramid states that after satisfying our physical and safety needs, the next most essential need for human beings is love and belonging.

It has been proven that without human connection, interaction, and love, humans cannot function well, and living without these puts us more at risk of experiencing extreme anxiety, depression, mental illness, and personality disorders.

The longest-running study on happiness, the Harvard Study of Adult Development, has been tracking the lives of 724 men since 1938. Researchers in the study have found that "how happy we are in our relationships has a powerful influence on our health," and concluded that people who are more socially connected to family, friends, and community are happier and healthier and live longer than people with fewer connections.

Research professor and author Brené Brown, who specializes in social connection, says, "A deep sense of love and belonging is an irreducible need of all people. We are biologically, cognitively, physically, and spiritually wired to love, to be loved, and to belong. When those needs are not met, we don't function as we were meant to. We break. We fall apart. We numb. We ache. We hurt others. We get sick."

It's clear that human connection is vital. But why is this so?

It comes down to survival. Our ancestors had to depend on and cooperate with each other to survive much harsher living conditions than we do now. Professor Matthew Lieberman explains in his book, *Social: Why Our Brains Are Wired to Connect*, that humans are the most connected of all living beings, and "what this suggests is that becoming more socially connected is essential to our survival. In a sense, evolution seems to have made bets at each step that the best way to make us more successful is to make us more social."

Have you ever felt physical pain after a breakup? Or hurt at being left out of a group? That's because social connection is so important that when we are rejected, we experience it the same way we would a physical blow.

Kipling D. Williams, a professor of psychological sciences at Purdue University, explains that "when a person is ostracized, the brain's dorsal anterior cingulate cortex, which registers physical pain, also feels this social injury." Proof that we are hardwired for connection.

Yet today, loneliness is a persistent problem. One in five Americans feels lonely or isolated, and this ratio increases to one in three after age sixty-five. More adults are living alone than ever before—over a quarter of Americans. Studies have found that loneliness is more dangerous than obesity and as damaging to your health as smoking fifteen cigarettes a day; it increases the risk of cardiovascular disease and shortens life-span.

I hope I've managed to convey the importance of human connection. If you've been feeling a little isolated or are missing the kind of meaningful relationships you'd like in your life, here are ten ways to find them.

1. JOIN A CLASS. Start a class in a subject you are interested in, like acting, meditation, or cooking; you'll be instantly surrounded by like-minded people—and potential friends.

2. FIND A WORKOUT YOU LOVE. Attending a workout class or going to a gym regularly is a great way to build a sense of community and see the same faces on a continuing basis. Open yourself up to connecting with others by asking questions and making conversation. Just saying hello to someone creates space for a

friendly chat. If there's interest, you can organize group workouts, such as a yoga session or a run, or suggest going for a bite to eat or a coffee after a session.

3. USE THE MEETUP APP. Meetup is a great platform for finding and building a community in your local area. From group hikes to brewery tours to coding classes, there are countless group activities for you to join, and lots of people for you to meet!

4. BOND WITH YOUR COWORKERS. The people we work with are often the people we spend the most time with, so why not make the effort to get to know them better? Organize something fun for someone's birthday, go for lunch together, share a personal story with them, or ask their advice.

5. VOLUNTEER. Volunteering is a terrific way to meet new people—and to feel good. Help at your local place of worship or in a local school. Many charitable organizations also offer volunteer opportunities, so check their websites or social media channels to learn about them.

6. CONNECT WITH PEOPLE YOU ALREADY KNOW. Good friendships take work and effort. They need to be nurtured, so take the time to build

a bond with those who are already in your life, whether it be the parents of your kids' friends, your hairdresser, or a friend of a friend. Suggest meeting up for a drink or a bite. Or reconnect with old friends. Don't you just love it when you speak to or see an old friend you haven't seen in years, and it's like you only saw each other yesterday? It makes you wonder why you lost touch in the first place!

7. PERFORM ACTS OF SERVICE. Do something nice and thoughtful for the people in your life. This doesn't always have to be expensive or time-consuming. You could help a friend with a move, or take dinner over to friends who've just had a baby. Simple, thoughtful gestures are often deeply appreciated.

8. TRAVEL. Travel is by far my favorite pastime; there's nothing better than being in a new country or city, experiencing all the place has to offer and meeting new people. Solo travel is especially great for making new friends, and while it may be a scary prospect to set off to a foreign land alone, just know that there are many people in the same boat keen to meet and connect with someone like you. There are also travel companies designed to bring solo travelers together for group trips,

so if the idea appeals to you, get online and book something!

9. BE INTERESTED . . . AND INTERESTING. When you meet people, be genuinely curious about them. Ask questions to learn about who they are. Listen; be encouraging and supportive. In return, be willing to share things about yourself. According to brothers Ori and Rom Brafman, authors of *Click: The Forces Behind How We Fully Engage with People, Work, and Everything We Do*, "the fact that both of you are letting down your guard helps lay the groundwork for a faster, closer personal connection."

10. SAY YES, AND PUT YOURSELF OUT THERE. After a long day at work, it's tempting to curl up on the couch at home and binge watch the latest show on Netflix, but needless to say, this is not the best way to form meaningful connections. Of course, time alone for self-care is important, but it's all about balance. Sometimes it can be intimidating to put yourself in a social situation where you don't know a lot of people, but remember, we're all human, and the people you meet have their own insecurities and fears. Start saying yes to things you're invited to, or if you hear someone mention an activity that sounds interesting to you, ask if you can

join them. Be open and be daring. You never know who you might meet!

THERE IS CURRENTLY a lot of division in the world, and while we are still hardwired to connect, we are retreating to our tribal teams, avoiding one another and labeling each other. We must find ways to reconnect if we are to survive. The three stories in this chapter will remind you how to do it— and how amazing it feels when you do.

There's the love story of Amanda and Adam, two people from different backgrounds who found each other through a game called *Ingress* and nurtured a deep, loving connection. Matthew Christian's story highlights how essential it is to be true to who you are and to be yourself with those you love.

But let's start with an especially timely tale—about two men with opposing political views who have put aside their differences to become the closest of friends.

KOUHYAR AND GREG:
AN UNLIKELY PAIR

America's polarization began long before November 8, 2016, but that was the day all hell broke loose. Donald Trump had been elected president, losing the popular vote but defeating Hillary Clinton in the Electoral College. Trump's supporters were stunned but elated; Clinton's were even more stunned—but furious. And so the dividing lines suddenly became gaping chasms.

I'm sure many can relate to having struggled around the dinner table at a family gathering as opinions fly like cruise missiles. A relative at a cousin's wedding may have scolded you for your beliefs. Have you seen a comment on Facebook by a coworker that infuriated, disgusted, or upset you? You are not alone. But believe it or not, two remarkable men found a way to put aside their differences and return to reason.

This is the story of a conservative Christian construction worker and a liberal Muslim immigrant from Iran, who, although they couldn't be more opposite, have found friendship and common ground that can inspire us all.

KOUHYAR MOSTASHFI, age forty-six, is a soft-spoken, studious, and thoughtful man. Born in Iran, he emigrated to the United States in 1994 for college. He studied hard and earned multiple degrees in engineering.

He married, settled in Ohio, and began his career. And along the way he became a US citizen. He had never thought of himself as a political person before, even though Iran's politics had long been turbulent. But for him, the process of becoming a US citizen ignited a passion for civics and democracy. Initially, he resisted choosing a party, but the more he learned, the more he began to lean Democratic. One big influence was the Bush administration's incursion into the Middle East after 9/11.

Kouhyar's research and experience suggested that the Democrats were more inclusive. Their worldview seemed to align with his own values, not only as a human being, but as a Muslim. He saw the Democratic tent as being large and diverse, and felt comfortable in it. When Barack Obama ran for president in 2008, Kouhyar liked what he saw and got involved with canvassing door-to-door.

As his political involvement increased, a friend suggested he join his county Democratic Party. Warren County, in south-western Ohio, was one of the most right-leaning counties in the whole state. Kouhyar became a central committee member and got his feet wet in grassroots activism. He campaigned for Obama again in the 2012 election, and in 2016, he supported Hillary Clinton's bid for president.

He endured the heated rhetoric and language—particularly strong in his Republican state—up until election day. The toxic atmosphere created by the election had caused this very mild-mannered man great distress, so he was glad it was about to be over. But when the election results came in, Kouhyar felt devastated and betrayed. He was so angry, he was ready to cut out everyone from his life who was anywhere close to right of center—friends, family, coworkers, people he'd known for years. Suddenly, they all seemed like the enemy.

GREG SMITH, age fifty-nine, another sweet, affable man with deep religious convictions, was born and raised in Waynesville, Ohio. A sleepy town of just a few thousand souls, one of Waynesville's claims to fame is their annual sauerkraut festival. Situated halfway between Cincinnati and Dayton in Warren County, it's best known for its gorgeous, lush open country and farmland.

And, as previously mentioned, its very conservative politics.

Greg grew up with three sisters and regularly attended church. Through high school, Greg found he moved easily between the different cliques in school—the nerds, the jocks, even the kids who were persistent trouble makers. Greg was a friend to all, and often found himself in the role of peacemaker.

When he left high school, Greg felt a need to serve the community, and chose a career in law enforcement. He served successfully for a decade, capped off by a run as local sheriff. But he eventually moved into construction, where the allure of a much larger paycheck was hard to pass up.

While construction paid well, Greg missed being in direct contact with the public, helping people solve their problems and settle their differences. His Christian faith had always been central to his life, regardless of his profession.

Greg's formal introduction to politics was when he cast his first vote in a presidential election in 1980 helping to elect Ronald Reagan. He was working for a Democratic sheriff at the time, and didn't tell his chief whom he'd voted for. When Reagan won, it was part of a red wave that swept out many Democrats, including Greg's boss. Though their political views did not align, Greg dearly loved the man and was sad to see him go. Greg resolved that, going forward, he would try never to let ideology interfere with his vote, and pledged to support the person he felt would do the best job.

So how did these two men, who seemed like they were from entirely different universes, get to know each other and form such a strong bond?

TO ANSWER THAT, let's go back a few years.

David Blankenhorn was born in one of the most conservative states in America—Mississippi—and went on to graduate magna cum laude from Harvard University, then got his master's degree, with distinction, from the University of Warwick in England. He founded the Institute for American Values, a think tank focusing on social and family issues. Though a liberal Democrat, David was so highly respected across the board that he was appointed by President George H. W. Bush to serve on the National Commission on America's Urban Families.

Decades later, David feared the election of 2016 would be an inflection point for America. He viewed the growing rift between the two sides with concern.

David's calling has always been uniting people, so not long after the election, he phoned one of his Institute for American Values associates, David Lapp, and ran an idea by him: to bring Republicans and Democrats together to try to find an atmosphere of understanding rather than one of vitriol.

The two Davids looked to history for a name for their organization. Given its mission to bring people back together, they felt there was no better example than Abraham Lincoln, a Republican known not only for installing rivals in his administration, but for steering the ship of state through even rougher waters than it's in today.

They looked to Lincoln's first inaugural address, where he spoke about the bitterness and anger between the North and the South that would soon lead to the Civil War. In it, Lincoln pleads with America's citizens to put aside their differences and embrace being Americans:

I am loath to close. We are not enemies, but friends. We must not be enemies. Though passion may have strained it must not break our bonds of affection. The mystic chords of memory, stretching from every battlefield and patriot grave to every living heart and hearthstone all over this broad land, will yet swell the chorus of the Union, when again touched, as surely they will be, by the better angels of our nature.

And so Better Angels was born, with a mandate to help depolarize Americans.

Their plan was to assemble people with conflicting beliefs and help them find common ground. The first group would be a handful of Trump and Clinton supporters, brought together in Ohio for a weekend workshop. It was extremely important to Blankenhorn and Lapp that they create a safe, professional environment for the participants, who had agreed to take a certain risk. They believed firmly that Better Angels should not be a forum to persuade anyone to abandon their core beliefs. Their goal was to humanize people to each other, despite their political differences. If change came, it would be organic, generated from within the participant and not through any outside force.

To establish ground rules and a format for sharing opinions, they brought in Bill Doherty, a noted family therapist and community organizer. He set ground rules, including prohibiting any accusations or exchange of insults during discussions. The idea that person-to-person and group conflicts be avoided completely was paramount to the workshop's success.

In December 2016, with postelection emotions still running high, the first Better Angels workshop convened in Lebanon, Ohio, with ten Trump supporters and eleven Clinton supporters.

What happened was an extremely pleasant surprise.

"We liked each other," was the participants' universal reaction. "We wanted to know more about each other. We wanted to keep on meeting. We wanted to help start workshops in communities all across America!"

Many participants in that first workshop had strong, positive emotional reactions. Some admitted to sharing feelings they'd kept bottled up; some cried openly, not out of pain or anger, but rather relief at finally being heard.

It clearly showed that Americans could still find camaraderie amid chaos and division. From there, the idea spread like ripples on a pond, with those former "enemies," the reds and blues, from the first workshop inviting their friends and families to another workshop to help cement the magic.

KOUHYAR GOT INVOLVED in Better Angels several months into Trump's presidency. David Lapp had approached the chair of the Democratic Party for Warren County and asked if they could put eight Republicans and eight Democrats together. It would be only the second such weekend workshop for Better Angels.

The chairperson put out the call for volunteers, and Kouhyar was curious. He had no idea what to expect. He'd been careful to avoid conversations with the many Republicans in his life since the election, but he was driven by a genuine desire to understand why people had voted the way they did. He signed up for the second Better Angels workshop held in late April 2017, and that's where he met Greg Smith.

When Greg first heard of the Better Angels workshop, he was intrigued and excited, because his first impulse has always been "How can I help?" His goal for the weekend was to help people understand his perspective, and where it came from. And, perhaps more important, he wanted to understand others' perspectives, too.

When they arrived, the attendees were asked to pick a partner and work on exercises as individuals, as partners, and then as a group. This gave Greg an idea. He decided to pick someone as foreign as possible to his own background and beliefs.

"I had a millennial to my left, a middle-aged Democrat next to him, and then a Muslim."

Greg chose to partner with the Muslim man.

Greg would be the first to admit he knew little about the Middle East—its history, its geography, the players in its conflicts. He felt that this pleasant man with the easy smile just might be able to answer his many questions. Kouhyar knew a lot about the Middle East and, specifically, about ISIS, a subject that was prominent in the news at the time, and he was all too happy to share.

Kouhyar was not only knowledgeable—to Greg's pleasant surprise, he was also calm, answering Greg's questions without making any accusations or talking down to anyone. Kouhyar was also very impressed by Greg, not only by his genuine curiosity, but the depth of his questions. At one point, Kouhyar asserted, "We fear what we don't know," which really resonated with Greg, whose religious beliefs taught him that we must face our fears.

Greg knew he'd chosen the right partner. Kouhyar felt the same.

OVER THAT WEEKEND, the two men realized they had far more in common than they had ever expected, like their religious convictions and their beliefs on affordable healthcare, a good education system, and responsible immigration policies. They got along. In fact, they really liked each other.

When that weekend ended, they knew they wanted to stay in touch. Being men of faith, they agreed to share the spiritual side of their lives with each other. Kouhyar attended Greg's church, and then Greg accompanied Kouhyar to his mosque—the same mosque Greg had recently watched protesters swarm around while he was building the adjacent highway. Greg came away far more enlightened and respecting of Islam.

Greg learned that Kouhyar believed in one God, just as he did. And they both realized that living their lives in a godly way meant acknowledging and respecting each other's faiths. They now break bread together, travel together, even pray together.

In June 2019 they carpooled to a Better Angels convention, splitting the driving duties. They had lots of passionate discussions, about music and entertainment and work, and lots of good-natured jabs at each other's habits and eccentricities. Kouhyar likens their relationship to that of brothers: familiar, gently kidding, but deeply caring.

As to the trust that's developed between them? Greg Smith has many lifelong friends, but he and Kouhyar have become so close that, as he puts it, "I have one friend that if I got in trouble I would call him at four o'clock in the morning. And if he didn't answer, I'd call Kouhyar at 4:05. So yeah, he's the second guy I'd call. Kouhyar is kind of a best friend now. I love that guy."

Both men admire the thoughtful design of the Better Angels workshops. The participants are taught to hear an opposing view, but instead of quickly framing an immediate answer and not really hearing what the speaker is saying, they're coached to examine the response and report what they've learned. The purpose is to discover which beliefs they have in common.

Another crucial aspect is the room allowed for self-reflection and self-critique. The process invites people to take a good look at their own opinions and express any issues or problems they have regarding their own side, in a safe place, without fear of reprisal.

They learn that one of the problems in contemporary political discourse is that people immediately assign each other labels, and make very generalized statements about huge groups of people that have been given those labels. Labeling is a shorthand method of vilifying someone you disagree with and is not constructive.

The first day, participants just practice listening to each

other, then break into small groups so opposing sides can engage in dialogue. By the third day, the groups choose projects on which to take action together. Kouhyar explained, "That's when Greg and I came up with the idea of visiting our places of worship."

GREG CONFESSES THAT, before Better Angels, he may not have been as good a Christian as he wanted to be. While he didn't accept Jesus as his savior until later in life, he always saw himself as a friendly person, but his concern for others was much more selective than it is now. In his younger days, while he "wasn't a mean man," he admits he also didn't take it well when people crossed him. He's long since let those walls tumble. He acknowledges that it's scary to be more vulnerable, but he now recognizes that the Christian teachings of peace require vulnerability.

One Democratic voter in their Better Angels workshop thought, before she got to know Greg, that he might be racist. That she was black didn't matter to Greg, who grew up in the sixties, when color polarized people even more than it does today. That she was an atheist didn't matter, either, as Greg accepts that as her choice. But he realized he needed to work hard to show her that he was not what she expected.

They are now dear friends. When Greg heard that she'd had a family tragedy, he immediately phoned her to see how she was and offer her his prayers, and to his surprise, even though she wasn't religious, she accepted.

. . .

BOTH KOUHYAR AND GREG stress that when talking to someone with a different political view, it's important not to question them in ways that box them in—with so-called gotcha
questions. Or leaving them no recourse by stating your own
feelings as an absolute. Or unleashing a shrill "How in the
world can you support that?" All these tactics simply widen
the gulf.

Kouhyar suggests phrasing your questions in a way that
lets the other person express what they believe. For instance,
rather than making an accusatory dig at them, try something
like, "I can see you support this person. What did you think
when he said such and such?" That approach shows your
good intentions, and that you're not trying to ambush or
belittle the other person. You want to understand their world
a little better, and if the other person feels safe, they will likely
give you a real answer, not a defensive dodge.

With all the strife permeating our lives, some might
be surprised by the foreign-born Kouhyar's assessment of
Americans: "We're tolerant, very tolerant. The blessing about
America is that Americans are very accepting, despite everything that we hear on the news." He feels strongly that most
Americans, deep down, want people to come to this country
and experience the amazing opportunities that exist here.

Greg agrees with his friend. While there are some on his
side of the spectrum who demonize immigrants, Greg, as he
has gotten to know Kouhyar, would happily see anyone from

his family in Iran come to this country. Greg has taken the measure of the man, and knows that anyone even remotely like him would be an asset to America. After all, that's the principle upon which the country was founded.

THE PHILOSOPHY BEHIND Better Angels is that people have more in common than they realize. But we can only discover those commonalities by engaging in constructive conversations and learning about each other. People retreat into themselves and their tribes in times of stress; we need to open each other up. The best way is to show sincere interest, and let the other person tell you their story.

When Better Angels began, NPR devoted an hourlong broadcast to them, and soon the word spread. Emails started streaming in from people around the country, asking, "Can you please come to my community?"

They did a summer bus tour in 2019, starting in, of course, Waynesville, Ohio, and ending in Philadelphia, visiting fifteen communities. They followed that with a fall tour starting in Washington, DC, proceeding through North Carolina, and ending in Nashville. In addition to holding their workshops, Better Angels has now trained 130 volunteers to moderate additional workshops in the future. Slowly but surely, wounds are being healed.

There's another, very unofficial chapter of Better Angels that Kouhyar and Greg both hope reaches the same kind of accord and understanding: the United States Congress.

TAKE ACTION

GREG AND KOUHYAR offer this call to action:

> '"If you are looking for the skills to have these meaningful and positive conversations with those you might oppose, join Better Angels. We offer a wide variety of workshops and exercises that will help sharpen your skills that could help make the world that much better for you and someone you have disagreed with."'

KOUHYAR OFFERS YOU a challenge and a final call to action:

> '"Using those tools from Better Angels, think of a group of people or even one person that you genuinely disagree with. Maybe even a family member. Start a conversation with them, using the respectful tools of discourse from Better Angels. You'll be surprised what you hear."'

LEARN MORE at www.better-angels.org.

ADAM AND AMANDA:
THE GAME OF LOVE

As we move into the third decade of the twenty-first century, it seems a good time to ask what kind of world we are living in, and what kind of people we're becoming. Today we all carry tiny, powerful computers in our pockets, allowing us to connect with the world in ways we could scarcely have imagined only ten years ago. But have they, paradoxically, also created more distance between us?

Go to a restaurant, and chances are you'll see at least one table where everyone is on their phone rather than chatting with the people right next to or across from them. Have our phones and computers so consumed us and commanded our attention that we've actually lost touch with each other? Have our little electronic servants so seized our minds and attention that we are becoming strangers, missing out on direct conversations, even losing something as simple yet reassuring as human touch?

That's one way to look at it.

But what if I told you a story about how mobile phones actually brought millions of fellow human beings together? Where they motivated so many to join forces toward a goal, not virtually but literally, face-to-face, hand in hand, creating real friendships and, in some cases, lifelong loves? What if you could download an app onto your phone right now that could change your life in wonderful ways? Would you do it?

For Adam and Amanda, that's exactly what happened, but when they first got involved, they had no idea what was in store for them both.

IN 2010 A VISIONARY entrepreneur at Google named John Hanke formed a start-up within the company. He called it Niantic Labs, in honor of the famous whaling ship *Niantic*, which brought fortune seekers to San Francisco during the gold rush of 1849. John had previously run Google's Geo division, with credits like Google Earth and Google Maps, and was fascinated by geography and cartography.

Niantic set about developing new forms of entertainment. Their first offering was Field Trip, an app that used the GPS in your phone as "your guide to the cool, hidden, and unique things in the world around you." Later they would create *Pokémon GO* and *Harry Potter: Wizards Unite*, but their first blockbuster game, in 2012, was *Ingress*.

Ingress is what is referred to as an MMO, or massive multiplayer online game.

It took the traditional concept of the video game, used primarily by stationary players, often played inside, and used GPS to expand the area of play out into the world. The GPS function allowed *Ingress* players' phones to "interact" virtually with real-world landmarks as the player followed clues in a game narrative based on a science fiction backstory.

Unlike virtual reality games, in which a player interacts with an electronic simulation of a created world, *Ingress* uses what's known as augmented reality (AR). AR blends the real world with technology, meaning players, known in the game as "agents," must go out and interact with their world. They need to capture and control "portals," which are physical objects or places of significance like monuments or statues, unusual architecture, bridges, and buildings. Agents find these portals using their phones, which act as a "window" into *Ingress* by overlaying computer-generated images over the real world.

The narrative of *Ingress* begins with the world's largest particle accelerator, the Large Hadron Collider on the French–Swiss border (a real thing), unleashing a powerful force known as Exotic Matter (fictional). Players exist in one of two opposing teams, the Enlightened and the Resistance, known in the game as "factions." The Enlightened see the powerful force as transcendent and good; the Resistance sees it as a threat to be stopped. When you first download the app, you must pick one of the two factions, and in order to level up, agents must collaborate with others in their faction to achieve their goals. People who play *Ingress* describe it as "a huge game of capture the flag" or like geocaching on steroids.

I was introduced to *Ingress* in 2013 when I was hired to play Susanna Moyer, a character who hosted an in-game show called the *Ingress Report*. I filmed more than 130 episodes, giving players important updates and news and reporting on big events in the world of *Ingress*. When I was hired, there was a lot of buzz within game circles that *Ingress* would be a hit. It went on to exceed everyone's expectations, and now has millions of players worldwide—including Adam and Amanda, the subjects of this story.

AMANDA HAD BEEN a paramedic since she was eighteen—over ten years. She says that much of what she knows in life, she learned in her ambulance. She saw "the best of people and the worst, and everything in between."

During one call, a quadriplegic patient required a routine move Amanda had done many times before. She and her partner were to roll the man off a bed and onto a stretcher for transport. But something went wrong. As they were hefting the man, they began to lose control, and he slipped. Amanda quickly shifted her weight in an unusual way. She kept the man from hitting the floor, but it came at a terrible expense to her own body—several herniated discs and a damaged knee.

The injuries left her unable to handle patients, and she lost her job in the ambulance. She worried about what to do for work, having only ever known one occupation, and at nearly thirty years of age wasn't sure who she was or what she wanted to do next. She almost panicked, but with the backing of her loving and supportive family, chose instead to take some time off to travel and consider her options. She had family in the airline industry, which made flying a lot cheaper. She spent a lot of time thinking about what made her tick and how she could conquer her fears.

Around this time, her older brother Geoffry mentioned a game he really enjoyed and felt she would, too. He teased her by saying, "It's super secret, and I can't tell you anything about it. You just have to download it yourself and figure it out."

He did not mention the game was science fiction, since he knew Amanda had no interest in that. Feeling low and looking for something exciting, Amanda decided to give it a try. Her immediate reaction was that the game was "conspiracy theory–esque," but she relented and immersed herself in it, joining a team in opposition to her brother's and quickly moving up levels.

Before long, *Ingress* had become an important part of her life. She traveled to Finland, finding her way around Helsinki looking for portals. When she found herself skipping coffee with friends to explore the city and play the game, which allowed her to discover places of significance she wouldn't have ordinarily sought out, she realized that *Ingress* was not only engaging her intellectually, it was a real emotional rush. She returned home officially in love with *Ingress*, and it was then that her gameplay really took off—leaving her brother in the dust, she told me with a hint of pride.

. . .

ADAM GREW UP with an absent father and a busy single mother so he didn't want to go to her with problems. He kept things to himself and didn't open up or trust people easily. His previous relationship lacked intimacy and Adam was more focused on other things, like taking care of his son instead of dating.

Adam came to *Ingress* a little later than Amanda, since the game's platform wasn't expanded to include the iPhone until nearly two years after its debut. But he got into it quickly, and was soon traveling outside his native Baton Rouge to meet fellow players, or "agents," in nearby cities like New Orleans.

Amanda had experienced her fill of "really ridiculously codependent" boyfriends, and while she had not sworn off relationships, she was cautious. *Ingress* turned out to be a great vehicle for meeting all kinds of people, but she was not actively looking for a man.

Amanda is also a very affectionate person. In fact, one of her trademark moves is to hug you before she even introduces herself or gets your name. She gets the important part—the human contact—done first, then moves on to the formalities. I remember her giving me many hugs when we met at various events while I was working on the game. She even half jokes that her "ideal job would be to give hugs and be really nice."

She'd get a glowing reference from me!

While Amanda and Adam were aware of each other through their game connections, they had not yet physically met—but that was about to change. Amanda had heard through mutual friends that Adam was a "pretty cool guy," and she was curious.

Ingress features group gatherings called "anomalies" where hundreds, sometimes thousands, of players descend on a city to play the game. It was at an anomaly in San Antonio that Adam and Amanda finally came face-to-face. They were staying with a larger group in an Airbnb, and they were immediately interested in each other. But they played it cool at first, going with the group flow, stealing the occasional glance at each other.

Amanda liked his purple hair and beard. Adam couldn't help but notice Amanda's warm mannerisms—her embrace of everyone she met and her engaging demeanor. Her evident affection for those around her was a powerful draw for Adam, who'd been bereft of that human connection for so long.

Luckily, it wasn't long before they got a chance to chat.

The group went to a Whataburger for a meal, and Adam made sure he and Amanda were sitting across from each other. The conversation got deep very quickly. One of the areas where they really connected was their shared feelings of social anxiety. Adam loved the gatherings and the proximity to so many new acquaintances, but being a true introvert, he often felt anxious in large group settings.

He mentioned this to Amanda and, to his great surprise,

discovered she felt the same way. He never would have guessed, given how easy it seemed for her to be in a crowd. She seemed born to mingle. He hung on her every word as she shared some of her secrets for dealing with her own discomfort in group settings, like putting on a persona to push herself to be more confident. As their discussion progressed, they both began to see many things they really liked about each other.

Back at their Airbnb, Amanda sat next to Adam on the sofa, at first careful not to invade his space. But when she offered to braid his hair, he agreed. She had a gut feeling that he needed human touch, and Adam really appreciated the moment and the connection.

And yet, when the anomaly was over and they all left San Antonio, Adam and Amanda didn't see each other again in person for three years!

In those three years, they both went on with their lives, but thought of each other often. They kept in touch through chat rooms, their mutual friends, and *Ingress*-related goings-on, so they never lost track of each other.

Then, out of the blue, on the streets of New Orleans, they saw each other again. Adam had just finished a GORUCK Challenge, which some *Ingress* players take part in during the anomalies. The challenge is modeled on a special-ops regimen where people perform difficult physical tasks while wearing weighted backpacks. It is particularly grueling, and wears its participants down. Adam was exhausted.

Amanda ran over and greeted Adam with a very extended hug. She noticed his heavy backpack and saw that he was in pain, so she offered to give him a back massage to soothe his sore muscles.

A few months later, Amanda found out Adam had a website that kept track of which player had collected the most *Ingress* merchandise, and she contacted him to see if she could get a mention on his site. That phone call lasted for hours, and they ended up discussing a lot more than merch.

They were each harboring growing feelings. Adam had never experienced such a deep connection with someone. While life had shown him that trusting people was dangerous, he didn't feel that way about Amanda. Just the opposite. Not too long after that phone call, Adam was asking himself if he was in love with her.

Amanda knew there was a real magnetism between them. Adam represented something warm and compassionate and real. She couldn't help but be drawn to him. I found it very sweet that Amanda had kept notes about all the times they had met up. Soon they were talking on the phone and via FaceTime several times a week.

But for Amanda, the thing that showed her unequivocally that Adam was the guy for her was a pair of socks.

Yes, you read that right, socks.

After a long day driving back from an anomaly in Florida together, they stopped at a friend's in Mississippi to spend the night. While they were getting ready for bed, Adam rifled through his bag and turned to her with a pair of socks in hand.

"Hey, it's chilly tonight. You need a pair of socks?"

Keep this in mind, guys, when considering flashy jewelry or expensive clothes or dinners to woo your love.

Amanda explained that while it seems quite silly, "like a really small thing," the incident with the socks was special because in the few weeks leading up to it they had shared some very intimate and vulnerable moments. One was when Adam confided in Amanda something he was really worried about and she promised to keep him safe. The second was when Adam watched Amanda in "a pure moment of joy" playing on the beach despite the fact that it was winter and cold out. The next was when Amanda broke down at a memorial dinner for Joe Philley, her good friend and a beloved member of the *Ingress* community who had died suddenly. While Adam wanted nothing more than to comfort Amanda, he respected her wishes and left her alone while she licked her wounds and slept through some of her sadness.

Adam's simple gesture to offer her a pair of socks said so much about how he thought and cared for others and was a culmination of a series of events that sealed the deal, confirming to Amanda that she had found the one.

And Adam had long since made up his mind. Once after they had had a small misunderstanding they talked it through and were able to quickly and easily straighten things out. Adam's response after they'd cleared the air was "wow, so this is what it feels like." He was referring to being able to have a conversation about a misunderstanding as apposed to it being the start of an argument and getting attacked verbally, which had happened often in his previous relationship.

Communication, consideration, and thoughtful gestures were things that mattered to both of them. They were, as Adam observed, "made for each other."

WHEN THE TIME CAME for Adam to pop the question, it almost went awry. While spending time somewhere "very special" to the couple (they preferred not to share the location), Amanda got cold and asked Adam for the keys to his car so she could go get her coat. He got very animated and refused to give them to her. Instead he made her wait while he left to retrieve the coat.

She was about to find out why he was so skittish.

He returned with the coat—and got down on one knee. He had her engagement ring with him, and the only safe place he could think of to keep it was clipped to his key ring. Taking the ring off, he handed it to her and asked her to marry him.

She was stunned. "I think I said something to the effect of 'Oh my God!' I just didn't expect it."

She delayed a few moments in saying yes, only because she was in tears and hugging him in joy.

I was overjoyed for them both. Amanda told me the big day was set for "Oh two oh two, two oh two oh." February 2, 2020.

That's some cool numerology.

I asked Adam if he had anything to add.

"Two things. Long-distance relationships are hard, very hard. And the *Ingress* community really misses you."

That last sentence really warmed my heart. I love the community, and while I am sad to no longer be working with Niantic, I am proud to have been part of *Ingress*. With the plethora of technology that seems to separate us these days, it's nice to know that some of it actually brings great people together—beautiful souls like Amanda and Adam.

TAKE ACTION

I'M A BIG FAN of the book *The 5 Love Languages* by Gary Chapman. According to Chapman, there are five ways to express and experience love: gifts, quality time, words of affirmation, acts of service, and physical touch.

We often show those close to us love in the way we like to receive it, not necessarily in the way they prefer to be loved. It's important to show people love in the way that resonates the most with them. Amanda saw that Adam had a powerful yearning for physical touch, and gave him that.

1. Take the 5 Love Languages test online at 5lovelanguages.com to discover which love languages are most important to you.

2. Read about each love language and its significance.

3. Have your partner and/or loved ones take the test, too, and learn what their preferred love languages are, then show them love in their preferred language. This is a great way to form a deeper connection with the people close to you—and maybe even improve your relationships with them.

MATTHEW CHRISTIAN:

TWO WORDS

A young man sits at his kitchen table, trying to focus on his calculus homework. But he can't stop thinking about what he wants to say, or *needs* to say, to his mother. All his life, this boy has kept a secret from his family, hiding a truth about himself that has caused him great pain and suffering over the years. Only two weeks prior, he first uttered the words to his therapist, and was pleasantly surprised by her nonchalant response. But he knew it was only a matter of time before he had to say those same two words to the people who mattered most—his family.

Finally giving up on his homework, the boy set up a camera to record his confession, hoping someday it might help give others in his situation the strength to do the same. But he finds himself too petrified to even speak. Instead, he hands his mother a piece of paper. It's a flyer for a camp, but not just any camp—a camp for gay kids.

Matthew Christian grew up in the middle of the Bible Belt, in Louisville, Kentucky. He went to Catholic school from kindergarten through high school and attended Mass two or three times a week, so the beliefs of the Catholic Church were well ingrained in him. Yet he knew early on that he would have to forge a different path.

Matthew recalls always being attracted to boys, even in kindergarten. One evening, when he was around eight years old, he was watching a film and found himself strongly drawn to the young male lead, thinking, *He's cute*. This finally put a label to the feelings, as he thought those two frightening words: I'm gay. As he told me, "In the Catholic Church, you're taught that being gay is wrong and it's not acceptable and that you're not supposed to question that. You're just supposed to change if you are gay, or at best not act on it."

Matthew also found it incredibly confusing, as the church preached compassion, love, and understanding, yet unequivocally told him that who he was was wrong. "It's awful because I've always felt that I was attracted to guys, so I knew I was born that way, but then having someone say the way you're born is wrong is such a defeating and very suffocating feeling, because you can't change it," he said.

And he did try to change. Matthew would pray every night for God to change him, but his prayers made no difference.

One thing he knew for sure was that he had to keep it a deep, dark secret. A pretty weighty burden for an eight-year-old kid, especially one who was already being taunted at school for "acting gay."

As time passed, he saw the trials and tribulations of other, older gay kids and even gay adults, and it confirmed his instinct for self-preservation. The world's blind hatred forced him deeper into his shell and he pretended to be straight, to avoid being attacked by bullies.

He practiced speaking differently to not "sound gay." He'd call his home answering machine and record himself speaking in as masculine a voice as he could, making sure to erase the recording afterward so that no one would find out what he was doing. He also worried about his future. How could he ever lead a normal life, find someone he loved, and start a family? At the time, same-sex marriage was illegal and seemed a distant possibility at best.

This was an incredibly lonely time for Matthew. He had no one to talk to about his feelings, and lived in a constant state of shame and silence.

Then, at seventeen, his parents gave him a laptop, and he started searching the internet to find out if there were other people like him out there. By his senior year, he was exploring a world he wanted to know better—through Myspace, where he met other gay teens and traded thoughts with them. It was comforting to know there were other teens like him, but he still felt like he could never be open—at least, not at home.

When Matthew went to college, he was surrounded by out gay men and women for the first time, and while it was reassuring to see them living open and proud lives, it was still tough for him to imagine one for himself. "I just felt really sad and depressed, and even though I had all these great friends and I had a really loving family, I was holding on to this secret," he said. "I was still trying to be something that I wasn't. There is this part of my life that I wasn't sharing with anyone."

Yet.

Soon he found an LGBTQ youth group at college, and gathered his courage to attend a meeting. "It was one of the best decisions I ever made, because it gave me this sense of community and that I'm not alone."

For the first time in his life, Matthew felt a sense of belonging to a group that really reflected who he was and understood him. He felt safe, able to finally be more like the person he felt he was, not the one he wanted people to think he was. He even met a guy, and they started dating.

As thrilled as he was about having this new, exciting relationship, it felt bittersweet, since he couldn't share it with his family and friends. To gain confidence and figure out what to say and do, Matthew watched YouTube videos of people coming out, and even watched over and over the "puppy" episode of Ellen DeGeneres's sitcom, *Ellen*, in which she reveals she's gay. He was looking for clues, models for how to come out and not to mess it up.

And so the afternoon came when Matthew could no longer put it off. He decided to start with the person closest to him: his mother.

Even though he knew his mother loved him, there was still the fear in the back of his mind that she might not react how he hoped she would. He'd heard horror stories of people being kicked out of their homes and rejected by their families after coming out, and Matthew was terrified this might happen to him.

Matthew decided to set up a camera to film his coming out to help give strength to those in similar situations. He wasn't the first to come out—far from it—but he knew from his own scouring of the internet that what he was planning could have an impact on another kid out there who might be contemplating doing the same thing and looking for guidance on how to do it.

His mother's response could not have been more perfect. When Matthew told her that he needed to tell her something, she softly asked him what it was. She gently coaxed him by asking if what he wanted to share was something about his personality, to which Matthew nodded his head. To encourage him further, she reassured him that whatever it was, it could never be something she'd "stop lovin' you for, hon. You know that, right?"

This made Matthew choke up, and to comfort him, she put her hand on his neck and shoulder. He put the flyer about the camp on the table. Finally it was out. He wanted that piece of paper to do what he couldn't find a way to. His mother's eyes scanned the sheet, and Matthew held his breath. The years of worry all culminated in this heart-stopping moment.

"What is this?" she asked, holding up the flyer. "I don't understand what it is."

Matthew shifted uneasily, alternating between a forced smile and exploding into tears. She looked him in the eyes as he tossed his hair and squirmed in his chair, now more like the seven-year-old she once knew than her nineteen-year-old son. "Is this something about you?" He nodded. He simply could not bring himself to say the two words.

"Well, tell me. I might know anyway," his mother said.

Matthew asked her to guess.

"Is it about boys or girls?"

He nodded.

She smiled gently.

"You gay?" The words came easily to her, but Matthew nearly collapsed in relief when she said them. She jumped up and embraced him in a tight hug as his eyes welled with tears. His mother, the person who loved him the most, had taken his hand and, for the moment, led him to safety by saying the words for him. She held him while he cried, and he knew that while this was just the start of a long journey, it would get easier to tell people.

Matthew sobbed and apologized to his mother, but she'd have none of it. "Don't be sorry, silly," she gently admonished. She showered him with kisses, telling him she just wanted him to be happy, to have whatever life and future would allow him to express himself and live his life with the greatest joy and authenticity. "I don't want people to be prejudiced. You're born how you are." She asked if his friends knew, and he shook his head. He was afraid to tell them.

"If they're your real friends, they won't care." As usual, mothers are wise.

"Her reaction made me feel a thousand times lighter,"

Matthew said. "That huge secret I'd been keeping for so long, this big, dark, horrible part of my life. And then for my mom to say, 'It's fine. Don't worry. I love you no matter what.'"

That moment changed everything.

THE VIDEO TURNED OUT to be a precious record of a tumultuous event Matthew had known he needed to record. But actually showing it to anyone took a while.

Nearly five years, to be exact.

When he finally found the courage to post his video, it went viral. Today, that record of his moment of truth has been viewed millions of times.

Matthew hopes it has inspired and helped many others like him. It's a sentimental reminder of how far he's come. "It's funny, looking back now and thinking of a time when I wasn't out. It's such an odd concept to me now."

While coming out was a real awakening for Matthew and has made his life so much easier, it might not be for everyone. All the things he worried about, the potential negative repercussions, can and do occur. When his first boyfriend came out, he was promptly thrown out of his house. Changing attitudes can take time, and some people just aren't ready for the news. Not everyone is as understanding and evolved as Matthew's family. After coming out to his mother, he told his dad, who responded in a similar way: not surprised, and completely open and loving. The same with the rest of his family—even an uncle who, it turns out, had been afraid to come out himself and was in a long term relationship with a man.

Matthew's lesson to you, naturally, is to be who you are, and come out on your own terms when you feel safe and comfortable doing so. Coming out, for him, was "one of the best decisions I've ever made, being me and letting everyone know it. And it's not just about coming out, but it's about being honest with yourself. I definitely recommend that everyone do that."

Matthew knows how impossible it may sometimes seem—he's been there!—but he guarantees that speaking your truth and living life authentically will feel worlds better than living a lie.

"There are always people who think they know what's best for you, and maybe sometimes they do, but it's important to remember that you know yourself better than anyone else, and ultimately, it's your life. You're in control of it. Make sure you're living for you."

TAKE ACTION

1. Think of something you have been hiding from someone close to you. Is there something you want to share and be honest about but haven't been able to? This could be coming out as gay, telling family you don't want to go

to college, deciding not to follow an expected career path, perhaps ending a relationship or talking to a partner about something new that you want to try in your relationship.

2. Plan how you will share your truth, where and when you'll speak to them and what you want to say. Share your truth when you feel safe about doing so and are ready to do so.

And remember . . .

3. Always be true to yourself.

PART 2

OVERCOMING ADVERSITY

I am convinced that life is 10% what happens
to me and 90% how I react to it.
—Charles R. Swindoll

S tarting with the ancient Greeks, many men have uttered some variation of the above quote. It goes to show how important it is to remember that we do, in fact, have some control over what happens when life throws us a curveball.

We will all experience pain, disappointment, and almost certainly loss and sickness. Yet some people respond by rising to the challenge, while others sink under the weight. What's the differentiator? I interviewed clinical psychologist Dr. Robert Puff, host of the *Happiness Podcast*, who speaks wisely about pain and suffering. He explains that pain is an inevitable physical feeling. However, suffering comes from the thoughts we have about the pain we are experiencing— for example, "Why is this happening to me?" or "I'll never feel good again." These thoughts are what cause suffering, and we can choose to change them.

After big setbacks or during times of misfortune, it can feel impossible to summon the mental strength to warrior our way out but when you're ready, there are things you can do to help ease the suffering.

In 2017 I interviewed John O'Leary for *The Uplifting Content Podcast*. When he was just nine years old, John suffered severe burns over his entire body and doctors gave him a 1 percent chance of surviving. No one expected him to make it. However, after dozens of surgeries and years of therapy and deep inner work, he is a profoundly happy, successful man with a beautiful family who inspires others through his work as a motivational speaker, author, and life coach. He feels that what happened to him was his greatest gift: the realization that, regardless of our personal and professional challenges, we can navigate and overcome to reveal a brighter vision. In John's words, "You can't always choose the path you walk in life, but you can always choose the manner in which you walk."

Here are some ways to help you deal with adversity:

1. Immerse yourself in uplifting stories about people who have overcome hardships similar to (or perhaps worse than) those you are experiencing. Knowing that someone else has made it through will give you hope that you can do the same.

2. Surround yourself with positive and supportive people. When you are dealing with a hardship, you need all the strength you can muster. Friends and family who are draining, negative, or toxic won't help, and can actually hinder your recovery. Spend time with those who are able to support, encourage, and help you through.

3. Take responsibility for what you can control in the situation. Some things will be out of your hands, so remember to change the things you can't accept, and accept the things you can't change.

4. Practice mindfulness. Let go of expectations, and pay attention to the voice in your head. Make sure the stories you tell yourself are positive and encouraging. Be loving and kind to yourself.

5. Use this time of trial as an opportunity to grow. Invest in yourself, read personal development books, or listen to audiobooks or podcasts about resilience and overcoming adversity.

While you've probably heard of posttraumatic stress disorder (PTSD), I was happy to recently learn about posttraumatic growth (PTG), a phenomenon named by psychologists Richard Tedeschi and Lawrence Calhoun in the mid-1990s. This new paradigm for finding one's personal strength explains how we sometimes experience positive transformation following trauma. "People develop new understandings of themselves, the world they live in, how to relate to other people, the kind of future they might have," says Tedeschi.

PTG suggests that we can become better people, wiser, and more compassionate, with closer relationships and a greater sense of purpose, not in spite of our trauma but because of it. Trauma can encourage us to reevaluate our priorities, become more spiritual, and change our philosophies of living.

Please understand that I am not trying to diminish the struggles you might be experiencing. I want to help you through them by sharing the stories in this chapter, to remind you that people are capable of great transformations, even—or especially—in the wake of tragedy. In this chapter, you'll hear about my good friend Phillip Barbb, who, at fourteen, had his life turned utterly upside down, setting him on a path of self-destruction that took years to undo. Hannah Power suffered an unspeakable violation that nearly destroyed her—until she rediscovered her strength and, bit by bit, reasserted control over her life. Danny Chew was a professional cyclist who became paralyzed from the chest down after an accident, yet battled against the odds to find his way back onto a bike.

While their struggles may not be exactly like yours, I'm sure you'll agree they went through extraordinary trials and came out on the other side. And so can you.

PHILLIP ANDREW BARBB:

FROM ALCOHOL TO ACTUALIZATION

Phillip Andrew Barbb was fourteen when his whole life came crashing down around him. He was having dinner with his sister and father at their home in a suburb of Detroit, laughing and joking at the table. His mother was in the hospital for what he thought was a gallstone. A few minutes into dinner, Phillip noticed the expression on his father's face, and he instantly knew something was wrong. His father walked over to turn off the TV, and shared the shattering news that it was not, in fact, a gallstone—Phillip's mother had an aggressive form of cancer.

All Phillip could do in that moment was cry. Shortly afterward, he put on a basketball jersey and went to play in his high school basketball game, trying to block out the devastating new reality awaiting him and his family.

I first met Phillip when he sent me a Facebook message back in 2017. He was a fan of Uplifting Content, and reached out because we both work in entertainment, live in LA, and are on a mission to inspire others. We met for coffee in Westwood, California, where he first shared his remarkable story. Phillip is a friend who always leaves me feeling more energized, inspired, and happy after spending time with him. He's the kind of friend everyone should have, and the kind of person we should all aim to be. And when it came to finding stories about overcoming adversity, I knew without a shadow of a doubt that I needed to share his.

PHILLIP WAS BORN and raised in metro Detroit, where his dad was a cop and his mother sat on the school board. He always felt pressure to be "this perfect kid . . . to be really good in sports, to do well in school. I became, from a young age, very performance-driven."

He was also the youngest kid on the block, which created insecurities. "I always hung out with a lot of older kids, so I was torn between these two worlds of trying to be this perfect little kid for my parents, but then cool enough, smart enough, funny enough to hang with the older kids."

When he was eleven, he started drinking to fit in, and it made him feel cool, "like I was part of the group." Alcohol also helped mask his anxiety about not being good enough. And as unorthodox as it was for such a young boy to be drinking, initially, it didn't cause a lot of problems. He continued to excel in sports and academics, making the honor roll and serving as president of the student council.

Phillip seemed to be managing his stresses . . . until he learned about his mother's illness.

Margaret "Marge" Barbb battled cancer for eleven months, and Phillip was at her side every step of the way— supporting her through chemo, watching her skin and eye color change and her hair fall out. Her final moments came just a week before Phillip's sixteenth birthday.

"I was at her bedside holding her hand as she took her last breath," he told me. It was this searing image of his mother's death that haunted Phillip for years and set him on a path of self-destruction.

While Phillip had loving and supportive friends and family, he didn't know how to communicate what he was feeling. Without the skills and tools to help him process his profound grief, he turned to alcohol and started drinking more and more often.

When a friend threw an innocent teenage ice cream social, Phillip says, "I'm the only one that showed up with alcohol."

He just couldn't understand why everyone made such a fuss.

"Never once did I ever think, 'I'm drinking because I'm so sad and hurt and broken and feel so lost,'" he explained.

Then things got very dangerous. Drinking and driving, sometimes speeding 100 miles an hour down side streets, he took to blowing through stop signs as a thrill. It was insane, but, Phillip admitted, "I think there was a part of me that almost wanted to get caught."

And it continued. "I was not only hurting myself, I was hurting my family," he said.

But try as they might, they simply couldn't get through to him. At eighteen, Phillip was arrested for crashing his car while drunk, and again at nineteen for drunk driving. While home for the holidays, he picked a fight with a neighbor and was so drunk, the next day he didn't even remember what he'd done. That was the last straw for his father, who told Phillip he was no longer welcome at home. Phillip was devastated.

But he kept drinking.

At twenty, another arrest. Yet in spite of this, he was still performing well in college. At twenty-two, armed with a new degree and determined to move to Los Angeles and reinvent himself, fate did him a favor and altered his plans.

Phillip described the moment it all changed.

"So I'm getting ready to move to California. Eleven days before I move, I get pulled over in the town where my dad's a retired police officer by the only guy that doesn't recognize the last name because he was the newest cop. It was just such a blessing."

Being arrested for driving under the influence sure didn't feel like a blessing at the time. But it turned out to be the best thing for him.

The court ordered Phillip to begin attending Alcoholics Anonymous, known to its more than two million members worldwide as AA. AA is a strictly nonprofessional organization that is entirely self-supporting and apolitical. The only requirement to join is a desire to stop drinking. Since its founding in 1935, the organization has helped millions of people quit alcohol for good.

Phillip was resistant at first. He told people he was being ordered to attend the twelve-step program, but in the back of his mind, he was relieved to be getting help. "In group therapy, you're hearing other people," he says. "You're realizing you're not the only one that has issues, and that was so powerful."

The meetings opened his eyes to the power of accountability and openness. Rather than hiding his feelings by drinking, for the first time in his life, Phillip discovered that sharing them with others could help him heal. "It allowed me to take off that mask I had developed and let people really see what was going on, and it was absolutely life-changing."

Delaying his move to California to deal with his DUI, Phillip kept going to meetings and, in time, began to understand his long-suppressed feelings over the death of his mother. Emerging from the fog, he turned toward leading a truly authentic life, the basis of the work he does now.

And he's quite candid about the process. "I didn't do everything perfectly. I've fought a lot of things in the program. It wasn't like all of a sudden one day, magically, everything changed. But it really helped me get onto the path I'm on today." He gratefully acknowledges, "A group of strangers taught me how to be myself."

. . .

A YEAR LATER, he was finally ready to make his move to California—this time with a lot less emotional baggage. A good thing, given how stressful this new chapter of his life would soon prove.

I can attest that moving to LA and making it in the entertainment business is no easy feat. It can be very hard to make connections and build a career. For some, it takes years, and for many others, it never happens.

Phillip had no contacts, no experience, and little understanding of the entertainment industry, but he did have (and still has) an unwavering work ethic. He took a series of odd jobs, from selling clothing to vitamins to deejaying. He answered phones at an architectural firm. He sometimes worked three different shifts in one day just to stay afloat. All the while he continued to chase his dream, constantly emailing and going door-to-door, cold-calling production companies, "telling anyone and everyone what I wanted to do." Which was to produce television.

He shared a one-bedroom apartment with another guy, both of them sleeping on air mattresses—not exactly the glamorous Hollywood life you'd imagine. But he pressed on, staying grounded with AA meetings and working to live a life of purpose, despite sometimes wavering on what that purpose was.

At particularly low moments, he reached out to his dad, asking, "What did I do? This is such a mistake. What made me think I could come and do this?" His father had always encouraged him to pursue his dreams, and was his greatest supporter. He urged his son not to quit.

And then . . . it happened.

Ironically, after all Phillip's hard work, it was a chance encounter while playing basketball in LA's Westwood Park that gave him his big break.

He smiles as he tells the story. "One day I met a guy named Kevin Bartel, who was looking for a TV producer. He brought me in for an interview, coached me on what to say, and I ended up getting the job on my very first show— *Undercover Boss*, on CBS."

And Kevin didn't just help him get the job and then disappear. "Kevin has now become a kind of mentor, an older brother figure to me, and we have worked on many projects together for various networks," says Phillip.

When Phillip isn't producing television programs, he travels the country speaking to high school and college students about his story, as well as about how to break into the entertainment industry. Phillip explains, "I can't tell you you're going to meet somebody at basketball, but sometimes you just have to trust the process, even when you don't have evidence of it working. That was something AA taught me. Sometimes you're not going to have it all figured out; you just have to work on what you can control."

Phillip has gone from strength to strength, working on shows for Netflix, NBC, ABC, and YouTube Originals (formally YouTube Red), and winning many awards. Yet he still had some unfinished personal business.

. . .

AROUND FIVE OR SIX years after he started attending AA, Phillip was at a meeting on Sunset Boulevard in LA, listening to someone speak about the death of a parent. The man's story led to a major breakthrough for Phillip.

The man was "talking about the death of his parent in a way I had never been able to talk about my mom. He described a door at the end of the hallway. 'You need to walk through the door, but you're terrified of what's on the other side,' and that was how I felt about going through the process of grieving for my mother. 'It's going to hurt, it's going to be painful, I'm afraid,'" says Phillip.

Phillip found the strength to walk through that door, and it brought back a flood of happy memories he'd not been able to recall since her passing. One certainty Phillip has about tragedy is that time does not heal all wounds. "Only work does. Working through things, actually grieving, does."

Phillip attributes much of his suffering to keeping his pain over the death of his mother bottled up. And he's not alone. People often shut down, probably because we live in a society where people—especially men—are taught that it's not safe to talk about feelings and fears, or even to express emotions.

Phillip now knows that as a young person, he didn't realize all the resources he had available to him after his mother's death. When he looks back, he can see how lucky he really was. "I had tons of people, teachers, administrators, family, friends. I had such a massive support system and I still felt alone, because I had made a decision to isolate myself."

Phillip understands the power his story has with the kids he talks to, since in many ways, it's his teenage self sharing it. "If we really want to serve each other, we really want to help each other, really love each other, then we have to be willing to give our stories first, before we expect other people to open up and give us theirs," he says.

When dealing with another's pain or tragedy, Phillip emphasizes that the best thing you can ever say is simply, "'I don't know what you're going through, but I'm sorry and I'm here for you.' That's it. Don't try to fix me. Don't try to make me feel better. Just have my back, and be there if I want to talk about it."

Over the years, Phillip has built a very fulfilling life. Television producer, author, presenter, public speaker, and life coach, he gets immense satisfaction from using the lessons of his journey to help others. He acknowledges that you grow by giving, and tells young people that they are already sitting on the answers to their problems. Yet he is still learning, growing, and making new discoveries.

Once, while doing a podcast interview, he was asked, "What would you tell your eighteen-year-old self?" His reaction surprised even him.

"I started to talk about this and I actually started to cry, and I just wished at eighteen, I really knew, 'Hey, you're loved, you're enough, you're okay, you're fine,' and I'd been told all those things, but I didn't believe them."

I think we could all benefit from reminding ourselves of those important words on a regular basis.

TAKE ACTION

ARE YOU STRUGGLING with something right now—depression, stress from work, worries about finances, concern for your health, loss?

Phillip's advice to you is, "Open up to someone close to you that you trust, someone you feel safe telling about something that's on your mind. Take off the mask, share . . . and be authentic. It can change your life. It did mine."

HANNAH POWER:
THE POWER OF HANNAH

It was a cold, dark night in the French ski town of Morzine. After an evening with friends, twenty-three-year-old Hannah Power set out to walk the five hundred meters back to where she was staying. However, the snow and darkness conspired to disorient her, and soon she was lost.

Three men in a car saw her struggling. They flagged her down and assured her they knew the friend she was staying with, and offered to drive her home. It was a small, close-knit town, so Hannah figured she could trust them—and at the time, she didn't have much choice.

Instead, they drove out of town. The mood in the car shifted, and Hannah suddenly knew she was in grave danger. Her mind raced, convinced that the men were going to kill her. But instead of her life flashing before her eyes, she found herself thinking of everything that was important to her—and all the things she had spent so much time worrying about that *didn't* matter. She had twenty minutes in the car to think about all the people she loved, and how devastated they would be if she died; how heartbreaking it would be for her parents to identify her body. The thought of her mother shattered with grief woke something inside of Hannah, and she decided she was going to fight for her life.

A RECENT LAW SCHOOL GRADUATE, Hannah Power seemed to have it all: intelligence, beauty, and the world by the tail. Yet life had not been a bed of roses for the young Brit, and she had experienced her share of loss and setbacks. "I got hit with a big death when I was twenty-one, which was my cousin Victoria," she says. Victoria was only twenty-nine when she died, two years after being diagnosed with cancer. Victoria was like a sister to Hannah, and her death "was the most pain I ever experienced," Hannah says. Victoria's death really changed Hannah's life, and Hannah made a vow to live her life as best as she could for her cousin, because while she couldn't bring Victoria back, she could "bring her positivity to life and live for her."

Treading new emotional ground, Hannah was forced to come to terms with the mortality of someone so dear. "I think I always had faith in the future, and that was probably my main thing that got me through everything when I was young. Knowing that I would get through this because nothing does last forever." I can relate having certainly used the old adage "this too shall pass" to get through hardships in my life as well.

Hannah got through her beloved cousin's passing, honing her coping skills and growing in strength while maintaining a sense of conviction that drew many people to her. However, what happened to her that night in the car in France was about to become the test of a lifetime in overcoming adversity. But first she had to survive the terrifying ordeal.

"I started to beg, I was crying and begging and I was telling them, 'You know I'll do anything. Please, I've got such an amazing life ahead of me, and I'm so loved.' It was almost like, in saying all these things, I was lolling myself for the first time. I'd never given myself that self-love. I had never believed I was amazing. Then I started to really fight—kick and fight—and I just kept going, which I think was why I only got raped by one man and not all three of them."

Refusing to go gently into that bad night may have shortened the attack and even saved her life. The men tossed her out of the car, barefoot, and drove off. She was alive, but her ordeal was just beginning.

The French police and hospital personnel treated her with disbelief and irritation, as if she were some foreign troublemaker, and implied that she had done something wrong by walking home alone after a few drinks. Hannah was shocked.

"The hospital was awful. They treated me like dirt," she told me.

Even worse, they informed her she'd have to submit to an intimate exam by a male doctor in order to file a case. She felt that the people who were supposed to be helping her were merely taking up where her attackers had left off. Feeling completely alone, she phoned her mother, who immediately flew over to France to be by Hannah's side.

"I said to my mum, 'This is not gonna define me. It's just something that's happened and we'll deal with it.'" While simple enough to say, making good on that declaration would prove to be harder than she realized. I asked how she got through the first days and weeks after the attack.

"I think it was pure relief that I was alive," Hannah says. "That's one thing that a lot of rape victims don't have—a worser-case scenario than being raped by a stranger—and for me that was the possibility that I was actually gonna die. What actually got me through was huge gratitude that my family, who I loved more than anything, weren't suffering."

In the months that followed, Hannah felt she was coping, undergoing rounds of therapy and trying to put that awful night behind her. But at around six months, she began experiencing alarming symptoms like flashbacks, uncontrolled rage, and growing anxiety. "That's obviously how trauma works. I got knocked over by what ended up being PTSD. It was like the first six months, I'd almost been in this bubble. It was just a survival mode, where I was working so hard to preserve the great life I'd built. You know, I had a really good job, great friendships."

In confronting the PTSD, Hannah figuratively put her foot

down. "I was not gonna let these men take this from me, so I carried on." But eventually, it began to catch up to her and overwhelm her.

Hannah found herself feeling utterly alone, a member of a terrible secret club she never wanted to join. The World Health Organization estimates that *one in three women* worldwide have suffered violence, sexual or otherwise, at the hands of either an intimate partner or a stranger.

Hannah turned inward, isolated amid the debris of an ordeal she couldn't share because no one she was aware of had gone through it. In this way, rape victims are akin to combat veterans who find it difficult to speak to anyone who has not seen the cruelty of war—but the terrible difference is that while war usually conveys honor, rape carries shame.

In talking to her doctor, Hannah discovered that the six-month "grace period" before the PTSD kicked in was quite common. Her mind and body had simply had enough of coping, and needed a rest from trying to manage the horror.

What she admitted to next surprised me.

"I momentarily stopped believing that I'd get through it. So I started to drink."

The drinking, she came to realize, was less a way to mask the pain than a tool to help her to confront it and work through it. "What drinking enabled me to do was just to go all into it," she confided. "It was like my body was telling me that I needed to just embrace the pain and zoom straight down into it."

The memories of that obscene aggression needed to be

called out, examined, and drained of their power to distress her. Hannah found that the effects of alcohol gave her the strength to face her fears and process what happened. "So I wouldn't advocate it for everyone," she says, "but for me, it was what I chose."

Hannah decided that moving to the island paradise of Bali would help her heal. It also helped rationalize the drinking. "I thought, 'I'm going to Bali. I'm gonna be super Zen and healthy and it'll all go away.' And then I did go to Bali and I had a big period of counseling in this time, and actually I told the counselor about the drinking and she didn't tell me to stop. I think she knew it was a coping mechanism." But the terrors continued to haunt her, so the drinking continued. Then an accident falling off a scooter left her hospitalized for six days with a damaged shoulder and a growing dependence on alcohol as well as the powerful pain killer oxycodone.

Soon after, Hannah flew to Singapore on a "visa run," slang for leaving a country briefly, then returning, restarting the clock on how long you can legally stay. During the trip, Hannah ran out of oxycodone, and the frightening withdrawal symptoms sent her into a black hole of despair. This was rock bottom. There was no more dealing, no more bargaining with her body and mind.

"That was the final straw. 'Oh my God, alcohol has got you here. You damaged your shoulder.' It just all became clear and I just broke down. I cried my eyes out and I thought, 'What am I gonna do to get through this alcohol thing? I've got a real problem.'"

In desperation, she turned to a loved one for help. "I

rang my brother, 'cause I literally thought I was reaching the end. It was that scary."

Regaining her balance, Hannah realized that the trauma from her kidnapping and rape had never really ended, so on that day, she decided to put the attack away for good. The day she chose for her rebirth? Appropriately enough, her actual birthday.

She found a book on ending alcohol abuse, *Stop Drinking Now* by Allen Carr. "It was an eight-hour audiobook, and I had eight and a half hours between Singapore and my front door in Bali. And I was like, 'I'm gonna listen to this audiobook and I'm not gonna drink again. I'm gonna be cured of this problem, and my life is going to begin free from this horrific addiction,' and that's what happened," she says. "And then I just spent a lot of time reflecting, reading, learning, understanding, listening to podcasts, talking to people."

Hannah knew she would always be someone who had been raped. "It's the worst club. You can never lose your membership, but you can choose to put it in the back of your wallet. I was never not going be somebody who'd been raped, but I knew it wasn't going to be my whole life, and I'd get through it because I have an incredible support system." She now counsels other rape victims about healing, stressing awareness and education, and works with a consulting firm to use technology and community to help better support rape victims. She also donates profits from her jewelry line, Sederhana Designs, to the UK's Rape and Sexual Abuse Support Centre; to date, those profits have provided approximately ninety counseling sessions. Hannah says, "The way I think of it is, our happiness, our fulfillment, is a muscle that gets exercised. I think that the more you can test that muscle, the stronger it gets."

Hannah realized the struggles she'd faced had been a gift. "I used to be cross that my family had had so much more rubbish than other people's families," including the death of her cousin Victoria and bankruptcy. "I thought it wasn't fair. And now I almost feel a sense of compassion toward people who have had it easy. Because if you don't know the lows, you don't know the highs. Also, if you don't know how bad it can get and still get through it, you live in fear of it."

That was her gift.

"I had the experience of adversity to get me through it. And I felt such a sense of duty to help people." Hannah knows how many rape victims feel: "Totally ashamed and in the wrong that you've got to keep a secret. People even whisper the word. And this word, it's like Voldemort, but whether you say it loudly or you say it quietly, it still exists. The more that we can say it and bring it to the forefront, the less time these people spend feeling ashamed on their own in their bedrooms, crying and drinking. They can tell people, and people know how to react. Now there's the awareness around it, the education around it."

Hannah advocates steeping yourself in positive messages, books, and the experiences of others who have come through great tests and proven more resilient, more able to weather adversity. She emphasizes to victims how important it is to get support in the first few days after a rape, whether through counseling or friends and family. Hannah had the latter, but desperately needed professional support, which she wished she had sought out earlier.

I asked what message she would like to leave you with.

"Two things. The first would be, if you're going through adversity, to never lose faith. You will lose hope when you're in pain, but don't lose faith. Faith in the future. You have to focus on that goal of reaching solid ground. The best way to do that is to be around people or to read content, consume content, watch videos of people who have been through hell and come back."

The second part sounds harder: embracing your pain or trauma. "When it comes, and it will come, you have to go all in to it. You have to let it, at times, completely take you over," Hannah explains. Allow yourself to feel the pain. You cannot ward it off forever, so don't fight it; let it do its worst, but remain standing through it all. It will pass. Know that in the future, you will be stronger because of your pain, not in spite of it. How you choose to confront it and use it rather than let it use you will illuminate your healing path.

Hannah says she wouldn't change what happened to her that night because she is grateful for the lessons it taught her. She believes in karma and hopes that one day we will live in a more peaceful world. She wants her work to shine a light on a subject that is still mired in age-old taboos. There are many victims—women and men—like her, and she wants to bring comfort to all of them and educate society. To that latter point, she looks to the famous quote: "The only thing necessary for the triumph of evil is for good men to do nothing."

She adds, " . . . and of course, good women, too."

TAKE ACTION

HANNAH SUGGESTS that you "find something that gives you faith in the future."

With that in mind, write a list of ten things that give you hope for the future. How can you better support those things? What can you put out into the world to ensure that they are still there five, ten, or twenty years from now?

DANNY CHEW:
DANNY'S MILLION MILES

Have you ever imagined losing something you can never get back, something that defines who you are?

Until the late summer of 2016, Danny Chew had never considered that, either.

When I met Danny, I warmed to him immediately. His directness and authenticity, not to mention his quirky sense of humor, were hugely endearing. Honest to a fault, he speaks in what I came to call "Danny-isms," often tagging the end of sentences with the affirmation "all right?"

Danny grew up in the hills of Pittsburgh, and fell in love with cycling in high school. "I started keeping diaries or journals where I would write down how far I rode my bicycle every day. I have these journals that go back to 1978."

Danny has Asperger's syndrome. Like many others with this diagnosis, he has an uncanny ability to remain focused on one thing. Danny's love of cycling was so strong that by college, he had assigned himself the lifetime goal of cycling one million miles. For perspective, that would require pedaling from New York to Los Angeles and back nearly fourteen hundred times. It was a goal more suited to Olympian gods than men, but Danny was up to the task.

He earned a bachelor of science degree in mathematics from the University of Pittsburgh in 1987, but by the time he graduated, he was already moving in a different professional direction. He soon entered the ranks of serious cyclists.

In 1985, he finished in twelfth place in the United States National Professional Road Race Championships, a 156-mile race in Philadelphia. He discovered that he performed better in longer races, and decided to pursue the Race Across America, a nonstop 3,000-mile race.

Considered the ultimate test for ultracyclists, the Race Across America is a brutal endurance test starting at the Pacific and ending at the Chesapeake Bay, and includes uphill climbs totaling a staggering 175,000 feet—the equivalent of six Mount Everests. In order to have a chance at winning, you have to ride hundreds of miles per day on little sleep. Only the bravest cyclists need apply.

Danny competed in the Race Across America "eight years in a row, from 1994 to 2001, and won it twice, in 1996 and 1999, at eight days, seven hours."

Most of us would find that a grueling ride in a car, much less on a bike. Danny told me he would hallucinate at times, and nearly fall asleep at others. Despite requiring a large support crew and an RV to tail him, the Race Across America offered no prize money, so Danny eventually stopped competing.

Danny's next quest, in 2009, was a round trip to Alaska with his nephew. That four-and-a-half-month odyssey covered a breathtaking 12,000 miles. Meanwhile, between races, Danny maintained his pace to cycle a million miles by his sixty-eighth birthday, tasking himself with at least a thousand miles a week. It was during one of these uneventful practice runs on September 4, 2016, that everything changed.

"Just after my fifty-fourth birthday, I was riding with Cassie, a Facebook friend of mine. I got, like, one of these dizzy spells, vertigo, like the room's spinning, when I was riding at about twenty miles an hour down a slight hill. I had no time to put my hands up or to protect my head like I would normally do. So I just hit the pavement headfirst with all my body weight, crunching my neck. The helmet cracked in about ten or fifteen places. That helmet probably saved my life." Danny recovered his bearings and went to get back up and continue. Only he couldn't move.

His neck was broken.

"The doctor pretty much told me point blank that I'd most likely never walk again." Danny was sickened, in disbelief. His whole life was built around cycling. The joy of the ride, the excitement, the wind in his face as the scenery flew by. He couldn't believe that was all lost forever.

When the full weight of what had happened dawned on him, he felt helpless and hopeless. "To have all that freedom stripped out in an instant, it was devastating. I mean, for a while I was even suicidal. It was that bad." The man who'd been so full of life and joy was considering ending it all. The road ahead wasn't just impossibly bleak, it was . . . gone. With 220,000 miles remaining on his quest, one million miles might as well have been a billion.

I asked Danny if there was any hope he might walk again.

"Pretty much no hope, no. There's maybe a thirty percent chance that if I live another thirty years, the technology could get my legs working again. But that's far-fetched, though. Right? I'm hopeful, but only time will tell, you know?"

Danny spent two weeks in the hospital, then was sent to the Rehabilitation Institute of Chicago for ten weeks. I wanted to know what pulled him through this ordeal. He told me it was the vast outpouring of support from friends, family, and even strangers on social media. His nephew started a fund-raiser to help with the cost of Danny's recovery.

Many reached out with stories of others who had lost as much, if not more, mobility than Danny had but had continued the valiant fight. This love lifted Danny's head above water, and kept him going. One woman's message in particular gave him strength. "She had a daughter who had been hit by a car, had a spinal cord injury, but she was even worse [than I was]. She went into a coma, and the woman eventually lost her. And the woman wrote to me and said I encouraged her to have the first good day since her daughter died. That brought me to tears."

Danny says, "I think it's important to hang around other people that are in a similar situation to you, like a support group. I now have a lot of friends that are paralyzed and reading their encouraging stories is very inspirational."

Katie Smith, a fellow Pennsylvanian who had been paralyzed in an accident eleven years earlier, losing function below her upper chest, had became a champion to many, including Danny, because she would not let her injury stop her from doing whatever she wanted to do. Katie had discovered hand cycling—done using a special hand-powered tricycle—and taken it up as a way to enhance her mobility, and urged Danny to try it. "She loaned me her hand cycle, the first one," he says. Taking up hand cycling, Danny discovered he could still hit the road, albeit not at his former furious pace.

Danny finds great strength in the Katies of the world. Her unusual attitude about her accident gave Danny pause, but also optimism. "She said if she had a time machine and could go back and prevent her accident, she would not do so, because her life has been so rewarding and rich since. I'm nowhere near that point yet, all right? I'm only a little more than two years out from my accident, but it gives me hope."

Another of Danny's hand cycle coaches is Attila Domos, a legend in the community. Attila was a rock singer until 1993, when a fall left him paralyzed from the waist down. Since then, he's become one of the rock stars of hand cycling. Danny admires Attila's heavily muscled arms and hopes to build up his own someday.

"Before my accident, I would actually ride with Attila, him on his hand cycle and me on a regular bike. Back then, he offered for me to try his hand cycle and I said no, I refused to do it." The irony is not lost on Danny. "Isn't that something? And then I had the accident and now I have to ride one."

Danny now truly understands walking—or riding—in another person's shoes.

"I always told people, if you want to appreciate your eyesight, try wearing a blindfold and pretending you're blind for just one day." Other advice that has helped him tremendously came from a friend, who Danny says suggested "I compare myself from the day of the accident to where I am now. That I'm a lot better now than I was right after the accident. So that's the key. Don't try to compare myself to what I could do before my accident, but take a look, see how far I've come since that day."

Despite his physical limitations, his spirit has come through stronger than ever. Danny has learned to adapt. As he explained to me: "Basically, only the top third of me works. I have pretty good use of my hands and arms. But because I'm paralyzed from the chest down, my breathing capacity is only about fifty percent of what it was before my accident, so I don't breathe as well and I can't sweat at all. I used to love riding in real hot weather, but now if it's much over eighty degrees Fahrenheit, the heat just crushes me. I've got to pour tons of water over my head to keep cool. I have a smaller temperature range that I can ride in."

Because Danny cannot feel anything below his chest, there are also physical issues that sometimes go unattended as a result. He was shocked when one doctor pointed out some nasty sores that had develop on his backside, a result of remaining in one position for too long. He has been dealing with the sores, and he's vigilant in monitoring them so they never get out of control again. "I want to get to work and ride over a hundred miles in one day, and I'll probably be there next year if I can keep these pressure sores at bay. I have to be able to use my own cell phone to take pictures of my butt."

His frank description of how the phone allows him to document the sores had me doubled over with laughter, but it was also a profound lesson. Danny reminded me that while pain is physical, suffering comes from the mind. Rather than dwelling on what he's lost, Danny considers how much he has achieved and grown, and what he is able to do now. With his eyes on the future, his suffering subsides.

Years ago, Danny Chew set a goal to ride one million miles. Then life threw him a very big, very difficult curveball. But Danny is a man of his word. Fate took away his legs, but it could not take away his dream.

So can he still get his million?

"Well, I don't know. It looks like not, with the current rate I'm on, because, you know, I'm a mathematician. I know numbers. I need to be doing at least ten thousand miles a year, and I'm not even getting fifteen hundred yet." Sure, he can do the math and knows those remaining miles are pretty intimidating, but everything looked impossible after his accident, as he lay in that hospital bed, unable to even wiggle his toes. Danny isn't slowing down. He keeps moving and looking for inspiration. And his friends continue to encourage him.

"There's another race called the Trans Am Bike Race. Forty-two hundred miles. This woman Susan told me about her husband. Retired, sixty-four years old. He was in Kansas riding this race and out of nowhere a car ran over him. He had a spinal cord injury like me. In the hospital for like, four or five weeks, and then he died. I've been writing to her, trying to help her cope with the loss of her husband."

Susan told Danny that "she would much rather her husband be alive and be in my condition, you know, like in a wheelchair, than not have him at all, you know? She told me to make the most out of what I can do, 'cause I'm still alive and I have my arms, you know?" Danny cherishes her words, and looks to them for comfort.

What message would Danny Chew like you to take from his story?

"There's always hope at the end of the rainbow. You know, I mean, as dark as things seem, positive things will always come from the negative things that happen to you. So if you focus on the positive and try to channel out the negative, you can have a positive impact on a lot of people, and that can be very satisfying."

Listening to him, I realized I haven't always appreciated it when people say, "Be grateful for what you have, because there are those worse off than you"—I would actually get annoyed when my mother would say that to me when I was younger. But Danny has a take on this adage that I find much more inspiring: to him, it's important to not let down those who look up to you.

"People are telling me that they look up to me for inspiration. I'm known for being persistent and not giving up, looking at the big picture. You can't let those people down who are worse off than you, because sometimes you're their hero."

He may not believe it yet, but I'm confident Danny will achieve his goal of cycling a million miles in his lifetime.

TAKE ACTION

FOLLOW DANNY'S ADVICE and take some time to appreciate what you have.

In a notebook or journal, write a list of one hundred things you are grateful for.

PART 3

ACTS OF SERVICE

Service to others is the rent you pay for your room here on Earth.
—Muhammad Ali

It is a strongly held belief of mine that we are here to be of service to others. Why? Simply because it feels so good when we do things for people. Why would we be programmed to feel that way if helping others wasn't essential?

There have been many studies on the benefits of altruism that strongly indicate it leads to lower stress levels, lower blood pressure, greater happiness, less depression, increased self-esteem, and even a longer life. This may explain why so many titans of industry, like Bill Gates, spend the first halves of their lives amassing vast fortunes, only to spend the second half giving them away. If nothing else, altruism can be a holistic alternative to taking pills, shopping compulsively, overeating, drinking heavily, or any of the other destructive things we sometimes do to feel better.

Being of service feels great and can make a huge positive impact in the lives of others. So if you're inspired to do more of it, here are some dos and don'ts for nurturing your inner altruist:

DO kind, generous things for others, solely for the purpose of showing your love and compassion for them.

DON'T always expect thanks, appreciation, or admiration . . . because sometimes you might not get it.

DO help those who want or need your help.

DON'T impose yourself on those who do not want your help.

DO ask what help people need; research and learn the best ways you can be of service to them.

DON'T assume you know more about what someone needs than they do.

DO give all the time, attention, energy, and money you can.

DON'T become overburdened or overwhelmed with helping people; you must take care of yourself first— or "put on your own oxygen mask"—before assisting others.

DO trust your gut; support and help the people and causes you believe in.

DO your homework: make sure the charities and nonprofits you donate to give at least 70 percent of the funds they receive to the causes they say they support. Check them out on charitynavigator.org or charitywatch.org.

SO WHAT CAN YOU DO? Tons of things! Here are some to get your cogs turning and ideas flowing.

TEN THINGS YOU CAN DO TO BE OF SERVICE

1. Say hello to, compliment, or smile at a stranger, and perhaps go so far as to do all three if you're feeling extra daring! But keep it authentic.

2. Volunteer at a nursing home. Read to, play games with, or entertain residents. If you have an elderly family member or a friend in a nursing home nearby, volunteer there as a way of spending more time with them.

3. Adopt a pet from the pound if you can manage a long-term commitment.

4. Volunteer at your local hospital.

5. Call a friend or family member you haven't spoken to in a while—someone who you

know would be happy to hear from you—and catch up.

6. Clear out your wardrobe and home and donate things to your local charity or thrift store, or give them away to friends.

7. Make a donation to a charity or cause you believe in.

8. Become a Big Brother or Big Sister. I've been matched with my little sister, Sysy, since 2014, and we have had a blast. It's been such an incredible experience spending time and doing fun things with her over the years. I highly recommend the program. Go to bbbs.org to learn more.

9. Become a mentor and share your business skills. A great site to check out is micromentor .org, where you can offer to be a mentor.

10. Buy a breakfast, lunch, or dinner for a person in need, or pick up the check when having lunch or coffee with a friend . . . just because. Enjoy how shocking this might be for them. When they protest, a good comeback is, "This is my kind gesture for the day. Humor me."

In this chapter, you will hear from four people, all of whom saw an issue they were passionate about and were

moved to help. You'll meet Doniece Sandoval, who, sad-
dened by the living conditions of people living on the streets
in San Francisco, is working to give them back their dignity.
Chelsea Elliott is a determined young woman who didn't want
other kids to experience the same loss she had, so she set
up a foundation to offer hearing tests and eye screenings
to thousands of students across America. Rola Hallam is a
courageous Syrian British doctor who regularly risks her life
to save others in war-ravaged Syria. Finally, Chad Bernstein
founded an after-school program in Chicago and Miami that
has helped keep thousands of kids off the streets by mentoring
them and introducing them to music.

I hope that the stories in this chapter will ignite in you
that desire to give back and make a difference, and remind
you that you and your actions matter. Oh, and, of course, to
enjoy that warm inner glow that comes when you have given
freely to others.

DONIECE SANDOVAL:

RESTORING DIGNITY ONE SHOWER AT A TIME

When Doniece Sandoval and her husband moved to San Francisco from New York in the early 2000s to start a family, they looked for a neighborhood that would reflect their own diversity. Doniece, a Latina, and her husband, a first generation American of Albanian and Yugoslavian lineage, eventually adopted a daughter who was a proud blend of Pacific Islander and African American. They settled on the Western Addition, a bohemian district right in the heart of the City by the Bay—it felt like a small town within a much bigger town.

The Western Addition was a true melting pot. The warm, friendly faces at the street fairs and art festivals and in the neighborhood's family-run groceries came in all colors. The Sandovals greeted neighbors and strangers alike, celebrated the Fourth of July at block parties, and felt comfortable enough to knock on the neighbors' door to borrow a cup of sugar.

The Sandovals fell in love.

Unfortunately, so did others. A lot of others, with a lot of money. And soon the real estate prices in the neighborhood started going up and up and up. And up.

With the Bay Area's tech industry minting fortunes at an astounding rate, a vast torrent of investment washed into the Western Addition, and suddenly the rows of charming turn-of-the-century Victorians were reenvisioned as modern Victorians, decked out with Carrara marble, state-of-the-art fixtures, and Sub-Zero refrigerators.

So prices went up even more. As a homeowner, Doniece appreciated the progress of gentrification and the growth of her equity—at first. But she knew that the skyrocketing property values would soon take a toll on those who rented, displacing what she loved most about her neighborhood: the people.

Some of those neighbors packed up and moved to less costly areas, but there were three in particular who didn't want to move, nor could they afford to. These neighbors, all three courtly African American gentlemen in their eighties, making do with small pensions and Social Security payments, were finally evicted, leaving them to take up residence in their cars.

Neighbors like Doniece offered food and comfort, but that wasn't enough. Not long after, those old men, who had trusted in the system and worked hard their whole lives, suffered the final indignity when their cars were towed away, leaving them nowhere to live but the street, because the waitlist for shelters in San Francisco was now thousands deep.

Doniece was devastated. She struggled to find words to explain the unfairness to her five-year-old daughter. She was deeply bothered by what kind of society would treat people like that.

Because she'd known a very different world.

IT WAS THE SIXTIES, and President Lyndon B. Johnson's Great Society, a series of policy initiatives meant to fix all manner of social ills, was in full swing. Doniece saw it all firsthand, as her dad led the War on Poverty programs in South Texas, where the family lived. Caring about others was in Doniece's DNA.

When she turned twelve, she got her feet wet in social service. She started volunteering at Head Start, originally designed as a summer school program to help preschoolers catch up on what they needed to know to start elementary school.

Doniece fell hard for the little kids in her care, for their sunny faces and big, ambitious visions. "But even as young as I was then, I knew that their chances of achieving those dreams were incredibly slim, because these children were basically living in what are called *colonias*, where there is often no electricity, no running water, and people have dirt floors."

This injustice continued to trouble her as she went on to college and a high-powered marketing career. When I spoke with Doniece, I quickly understood why she was so successful in the business world. Concise and articulate, she says exactly what she means. But there's also a warmth and maternalism in her voice. I was touched by how she referred to people throughout our interview as "unhoused" instead of "homeless." That told me a lot about her, especially that she sees the humanity in everyone. And when she eventually moved from New York to San Francisco, the stirring to help others she had first felt as a child still welled strongly in her heart.

One day, not long after moving to San Francisco, Doniece hopped in a cab that took her to the most unbalanced part of the city. Little did she know that that ride would change her life—and, subsequently, the lives of many others.

Passing through the Tenderloin district, a blur of high-density housing and furious commerce set against San Francisco's strongest epidemic of destitution, Doniece could scarcely believe her eyes. She took in the teeming crowds of people living on the streets. "As we hit a particular corner, the cabdriver leaned over his shoulder and said, 'Welcome to the Land of Broken Dreams.' As I looked at the people, the first thought I had was that not a single one of them, when they were little, ever dreamed of growing up to be living on the streets. And it really hit me hard, because my adopted daughter was five, had come from the foster care system, and her life could have been very, very similar."

It was in that moment that Doniece knew she was going to take action. The drive was as strong as anything she'd ever felt in business. All she had to do was figure out what that action would be. "I just kept thinking about how similar those people were to me. We have this perception that they're nothing like us, but in truth, we all have the same hopes and dreams and fears."

With the seed of motivation planted, all Doniece needed was a direction. It didn't take long for her to find one—something uncomplicated yet incredibly powerful.

On her way home one afternoon, she passed a young woman living on the street. Doniece acknowledged her, as she tried to do with everyone, but it was what the woman said that struck her: "She kept saying over and over again that she would 'never be clean.'"

Doniece truly believes that when you seek something, the universe will often provide an answer. She also admits to being a bit of a clean freak who loves showers, so the young lady's anxiety resonated in her mind.

She asked herself, what if you couldn't get access to a shower on a regular basis? Could you keep a job? Could you apply for housing? She realized how the simple lack of basic personal care could keep you trapped where you were, unable to escape the despair of life on the street.

An idea started germinating. On the computer that evening, Doniece did some research, and was appalled by what she found. She turned up statistics that left her asking, "How can that be?" She discovered that for the more than seven thousand men, women, and children who lived on the streets at that time, there were only sixteen public shower stalls and about as many toilets. She was stunned and more than a little outraged, because she also knew that San Francisco was absurdly affluent, with 107 millionaires per square mile and another seventy-five billionaires in the city on top of that. "And yet we have third-world conditions available to people who are unhoused," she told me dejectedly.

A few days later, she saw an article in the *San Francisco Chronicle* that got her wheels turning. The federal government was about to hand the city millions of dollars to replace their old diesel buses. As a marketing guru, Doniece had to smile at the irony of her forming notion: "Wouldn't it be great to do something good with something people love to hate?"

That object of disdain was the classic city bus.

Knowing little about buses, she did know that rock stars used tour buses, and those buses absolutely *always* had bathrooms and showers.

What if . . . ?

Doniece knew her idea made sense if you connected all the dots, but she was well aware that there were a lot of dots to connect. She knew that taking obsolete buses and essentially turning them into mobile bathrooms to service those living on the streets was a good idea, maybe even a terrific one, but she expected quite a bit of resistance.

I'm not surprised that the brilliance of her concept—and, perhaps even more so, the power of her persuasion—made the sale. While she did encounter some initial resistance with the mayor's liaison, he later became a staunch ally, after she proved to him she wasn't going to be put off. The bureaucrats and government agencies were no match for Doniece Sandoval. But their reactions also pleasantly surprised her: they essentially said, "You go do it and we'll figure out how to make that happen."

Doniece was elated that her idea was clicking with the people whose help she needed. Now came the hard part: How do you take broken-down old buses with rows of uncomfortable seats and panoramic polycarbonate windows, and make them into inviting, private bathrooms?

You need a designer. A very talented and creative designer.

The noted Italian architect Renzo Piano had just completed the city's striking California Academy of Sciences, one of the first official LEED-certified buildings in the city. Doniece phoned Piano, pitched her idea, and immediately won him over. One day, after a few development meetings, they both started laughing as they simultaneously realized they had not spoken to a single potential end user of the service. So they took to the streets, talking to people about their wish lists. They even had a few organizations convene focus groups. The list was long, but there were three things they heard over and over again.

The first was that when you're unhoused, you live your life in the public eye without a moment of privacy. The next was that if you were a woman or LGBTQ, your chances of getting attacked in a public shower were incredibly high. The last was big: around 62 percent of the unhoused population had some form of disability.

Putting it all together, Doniece knew they needed a safe facility that was accessible to the disabled. When they realized those parameters didn't fit her original plan of six showers and one bathroom per bus, they went back to the drawing board. "We scrapped that, and decided we would use the two bus entrances to create two totally private bathrooms. The front unit had a wheelchair lift."

The next consideration was the user experience. The team wanted to give their guests VIP treatment, because they realized that *how* you served people was even more important than the service itself. "When you go to the Department of Motor Vehicles, it's a pretty wretched experience. However, if you are fortunate enough to go to a five-star hotel, the way you're treated makes you feel special. And if you go back, they begin to recognize you. They know your name, and you start to build this connection and feel really seen."

Doniece was aware of the lift to the spirit she was offering. "Access to a shower reconnects you with your sense of self-worth and with dignity, because dignity is both how you feel about yourself and how people treat you. When you're clean, you're less likely to be scorned and disregarded by the rest of society."

They would eventually refer to this concept as "radical hospitality," because as Doniece explained, "we meet people where they are by bringing our services to the street, which in and of itself is a profound act of care, and because of that they become like family to us."

They researched what paint color was best for their mobile units (blue, it turned out), installed skylights, and even gave them speakers to fill the space with music. High-end manufacturer Kohler heard about the project and offered whatever fixtures they needed. They found a company in Sacramento to build the prototype on which future buses would be modeled.

Then came the moment of truth. After putting all this together . . . would people understand what it was? Would people use it? Would people *like* it?

Doniece tells the story: "So, opening morning, there were two gentlemen who stood at the door, and they were a little hesitant to get on. They only spoke Spanish. They didn't realize I spoke Spanish, and they were talking to each other saying, 'You know, this is really weird. I don't know if I want to do this.'"

But, having not showered in so long, they gave in. "Fifteen minutes later, they emerged with massive Cheshire Cat grins on their faces, and I knew we were onto something good."

And with that, Doniece's brainchild, Lava Mae (a variation of the Spanish word for "wash me"), was a working, proven concept.

MORE THAN SIX YEARS LATER, Lava Mae has gone far beyond its original reconditioned transit buses. Now expanded to both Los Angeles and the East Bay, Lava Mae has provided upward of seventy thousand showers to nearly twenty thousand guests. They also have created thirty-one pop-up Care Villages, teaming with between fifteen and twenty-one other nonprofits and private and public sector partners to provide the unhoused with all kinds of necessities, from haircuts to legal advice.

Doniece is a huge believer in the "ripple effect," as she likes to call it.

Referring to the well-known quote, "I alone cannot change the world, but I can cast a stone upon the waters to create many ripples," Doniece says, "I know that Lava Mae is this ambitious, big undertaking, but when I step back and look at the ripple effects that it's made, it's powerful."

But she also knows that one does not need to take giant steps or start organizations to make a difference in the lives of others. A seventy-nine-year-old retired school teacher in Doniece's neighborhood illustrated to her that even simple acts of service matter. "Every morning she walks three kids in the neighborhood to school, then meets them after, takes them home, and does their homework with them. She's been doing this so long, some of these kids are graduating from high school and going on to college."

Of course, extraordinary impact often comes at a cost for its creator. Doniece admits it's been an emotional roller coaster. "I would say this time last year, I was pretty close to completely just falling apart, emotionally imploding. It's a lot to shoulder. I have twenty-seven employees whose livelihoods I'm responsible for. So it's incredibly stressful."

It's particularly tough on Doniece and her team when they get immersed in the lives of their guests, whose stories can be gut-wrenching. But other stress comes from the community itself, where NIMBYism ("not in my backyard") and often simple cruelty are rampant.

"On a regular basis, people walk by and say to us, 'How dare you use my tax dollars to wash these animals?'" Doniece says. She and her team patiently explain that the bathrooms are privately funded and don't use any government money.

Luckily, it's all worth it when people step out of the showers with the almost universal reaction, "I feel like a million bucks."

HOW DOES DONIECE suggest you can make a difference? She has one last story that might inspire you.

When Doniece was a child, it was commonly accepted that when you passed people on the street, you acknowledged them with a nod, a smile, and a hello. Sadly, it seemed to her that amid the bustle of San Francisco, people worked hard to ignore each other. So about two years ago, Doniece decided she was going to change that dynamic and get back to her roots.

Instead of just passing people, "I started this little experiment to see what would happen, and if it would make me feel more connected to the city. I started saying, 'Good morning.'" Sometimes she merely smiled, and it filled her with joy when people responded in kind. "I think we were all yearning to make that connection."

One morning, as she walked out of a deli, coffee in hand, she saw an unhoused a woman sitting on the sidewalk with her little dog, her belongings strewn around her. As Doniece got closer, she called out her usual "good morning," and noticed that the woman seemed startled. "So I stopped and stood in front of her, and she said, 'You see me?' I said, 'Yes, you're sitting right there.'"

What happened next took Doniece by surprise. The woman's eyes welled with tears as she said, "I thought I was a ghost. You are literally the first person in an entire week to acknowledge my presence."

Doniece was deeply moved by the woman's confession. She had read psychology studies that suggested that when most of us pass unhoused people on the street, our brains often don't recognize them as human beings. As Doniece puts it, "Even witnessing another person's existence is a tremendous gift that we just take for granted."

It was another universal sign showing Doniece that what she was doing wasn't just the right thing to do, it was the human thing to do.

TAKE ACTION

1. The next time you pass an unhoused person on the street, smile and say hello; show them that you see them and acknowledge that they exist. This simple act can help give someone back their dignity and improve their sense of self-worth.

2. Decide now to do something to make a difference in someone's life, even if it only takes a few minutes. As Doniece would tell you, "That ripple effect, however tiny? You have no idea how far it can go."

CHELSEA ELLIOTT:

HALF HELEN,
FULL HEART

The world of a small child is so big, so colorful, so . . . new. You never know what sights, sounds, smells, tastes you're about to discover. Everything is fresh and original. But when everything is happening for the first time, it's also likely you don't realize what you're missing.

So it was with Chelsea Elliott.

A happy toddler back in 1994, Chelsea had no idea that Texas governor Ann Richards had just signed legislation requiring all preschools and day care centers to conduct vision and hearing tests. Chelsea was among one of the first groups screened. Afterward, her mother received a disturbing phone call from the woman who had conducted the vision test.

"I am not a nurse," the woman said in a somber tone,

"but there's something wrong with her left eye. I don't know what it is, but Chelsea needs to see a doctor immediately."

Alarmed, Chelsea's mother turned to a fellow member of the Lions Club, an international organization whose motto is literally "We Serve." In 1925 Helen Keller, who had lost both her sight and her hearing from a childhood illness and had become one of the most famous deaf-blind people in history, challenged the Lions Club to become "Knights of the blind in the crusade against darkness." From that time on, vision care and programs for the blind became large components of the Lions Club's mandate.

The Lions member Chelsea's mother contacted was an optometrist. The man did a very quick examination of Chelsea and, after just a few minutes, turned to her mother and delivered the terrible news: "She's completely blind in her left eye." Not only that, he added, he'd never seen that type of disease before, and Chelsea needed to be examined by experts.

Immediately.

A team of specialists frantically tried to understand the perplexing condition plaguing the otherwise happy little girl. But other than concluding the blindness seemed irreversible, they were stumped.

"Over the next four days, I had appointments with six different doctors to rule out retinoblastoma, a cancer that begins in the retina," Chelsea told me. "And on day four, we ended up in the office of a twenty-eight-year-old retina surgeon who had just moved to Austin. My mom jokingly called him Doogie Howser."

His real name was José "Pepe" Martinez, and while he may have been young, he managed to do what the other physicians had not: provide a diagnosis for Chelsea's condition. Dr. Martinez quickly determined that Chelsea had Coats disease, a virus of the retina that causes the tiny blood vessels in the back of the eye to rupture. The buildup of lipids from the blood become trapped in the layers of tissue of the retina, eventually detaching the retina and causing the functional portion of the retina at its center to atrophy.

While Coats disease can sometimes be stopped and the damage contained, for Chelsea, it had been diagnosed too late. On top of the traumatic diagnosis, Dr. Martinez insisted that they schedule surgery right away to stop the hemorrhaging.

Young Chelsea was terrified. She told the doctor she was afraid he might take out her eye, which he patiently explained he wouldn't.

After Chelsea's procedure, the OR nurse forgot to warn her parents not to let her lie down because it would dramatically increase the swelling. "So the first thing my parents did was take me home and lay me down to rest," Chelsea says.

By Chelsea's follow-up appointment the next day, her eye had completely swollen shut, making it look like it had indeed been removed. "At four I didn't really understand what was going on. So I saw myself in the mirror and looked questionably at Dr. Martinez and said, 'You took out my eye!'"

The young surgeon was overcome with emotion, Chelsea remembers. "He wrapped his arms around me and, with tears in his eyes, told me, 'No, I promise. It's still there.'"

HAVING SUFFERED the ordeal of an operation, Chelsea, at six, was beginning to understand that she was not quite like everyone else. And there was more bad news coming.

Chelsea's September birthday meant she had missed the hearing test mandated by the state the year before. Now, two years after the issues with her eye had surfaced, her ears were tested, and it was discovered that she had *no hearing at all* in her right ear. Her pediatric ear, nose, and throat doctor surmised that as an infant, a series of ear infections in her right ear might have caused two of the three bones in her middle ear to literally dissolve, rendering her deaf in that ear.

Fortunately, her youth allowed her to adapt and even thrive. Chelsea admits that she was a handful as a child. "Nothing stopped me. Not even the first ten nos. I had this wild, audacious personality. Ask my mom, and she'd say I was a borderline hellion." This is hard to imagine of the gentle, determined woman I interviewed, but it was likely this same force of personality that got her through the trying years to come.

As a young teen, Chelsea began to face a new set of concerns. Her appearance was suddenly quite important to her, and by middle school, her affected eye had begun to atrophy and change, both shrinking and developing a prominent silvery cataract. "Since I was four, I'd always known that I would have to have my eye removed at some point," she told me. And she realized there was no avoiding it anymore.

And so, in the summer before her sophomore year, Chelsea met with her retina surgeon to discuss the medical process, called enucleation. The six-week healing time before she could receive a prosthetic eye meant she'd have to spend at least two weeks wearing an eye patch to school. She worried about how she'd look after the surgery, and later, in her prom and graduation photos. That trepidation—along with a million others—dominated her thoughts as she checked into the hospital.

The operation went well, but after the procedure, her surgeon warned her, "Whatever you do, don't look in the mirror." But like most people do when told not to do something, she did exactly that—and was horrified. "My eyelid had been stitched shut to allow the socket to heal, and I knew it was to remain stitched for six weeks, but just seeing that, a sense of fear encompassed me."

She felt a crashing sense of despair and profound regret. "What have I done?" she kept repeating to herself. She dreaded returning to school wearing an eye patch. As she anxiously walked through the front doors on her first day back, all Chelsea wanted to do was disappear. Stepping inside her class and holding her breath, she was overwhelmed to find all of her tenth-grade friends waiting for her . . . every single one of them wearing an eye patch to show their support. And yet as loving as the gesture was, it still left her feeling different, apart. "I appreciated it. But at that time, all I wanted was to become invisible. I didn't want anyone to see me. I just wanted to wall myself off from the world and heal. Because I felt so broken."

Once she had healed, it was time to be fitted with an artificial eye. Luckily the process wasn't at all traumatic. She met with an ocularist, a highly trained professional who fits, fabricates, and paints prosthetic eyes. Chelsea's ocularist also works with the US Army to create artificial eyes for soldiers who have lost theirs in combat. She isn't just a medical professional, but also a gifted artist, who literally paints the details of the eye onto the prosthesis with such precision that it's nearly impossible to tell it's not a real eye.

Using Chelsea's other eye as a guide, "she asked me to bring the three most common colors in my closet, because of the way our irises tend to change color based on what color we wear," Chelsea explains.

NO MATTER HOW realistic Chelsea's new eye looked, teens can be cruel—even when they're trying to be "helpful," like the friend who told Chelsea that her new artificial eye didn't look any better than her "old eye." Chelsea had always been able to maintain a positive outlook, but now she found her anger slowly building.

At such a vulnerable, sensitive age, the stress of dealing with unwanted attention and comments about her eye caused her to internalize her emotions. She grew so anxious that her face would break out in what she referred to as "horrible" acne.

She was surrounded by well-meaning friends and family, but she just wanted to be left alone.

College, and particularly a semester abroad in France, was her chance to reinvent herself—and test out who else she might want to be. It also forced her to confront her past. A professor challenged her to put her story down on paper, something she fought "tooth and nail" to avoid doing, she told me. It was just too painful. But her professor insisted, and she finally wrote it down—everything from the time she lost her vision to what happened after the surgery that took her eye. Documenting her harrowing journey was powerfully cathartic and it gave her a perspective on the true power of her own story.

Chelsea wanted to use her experience to serve her community, she just wasn't sure how.

Later that year, she and her mother attended a local Lions Club meeting, where a speaker from a company called PediaVision introduced a device called the Welch Allyn Spot vision screener, a high-tech camera for detecting issues in children's vision. As the man described how it worked, Chelsea and her mother were moved to tears. The speaker noticed the women crying and asked, "Is everything okay?"

Chelsea quietly answered, "Had this device been around when I was little, it could have saved my vision." Her old anger welled up again. "I grumbled about it for a couple days, and then my mom, in her infinite wisdom, finally said, 'Shut up and go do something about it.'"

So Chelsea did. She reached out to the Lions Club and asked for an eight thousand dollar grant, which she received. Combining the grant with her graduation gift money, she bought a Spot camera and an audiometer, a device used to test hearing, and started a nonprofit foundation to provide vision and hearing screenings. Because she "was going to make sure that no other child went through the pain and the hurt that I suffered."

She called her nonprofit foundation Half Helen, inspired by the legendary Helen Keller. "I'm half blind, half deaf. I was half Helen," she explained.

WITH HER NEW EQUIPMENT and a burning desire to help, Chelsea focused her efforts on local schools. Despite the Texas bill requiring vision and hearing screenings, schools in the state weren't required to have a school nurse, and without nurses or volunteers to conduct the tests they were out of luck.

Chelsea's offer to these schools was simple: "Can I come use this new equipment and technology to screen your students?"

Chelsea became a one-woman show, screening two schools a week. She made great progress, but soon discovered Texas laws only allowed her to screen children up to four years old. She needed a way to reach a wider age group.

One of the eight US states that did not mandate school vision or hearing testing was Hawaii, so she packed her bags and equipment and went.

Chelsea knew she had something important to offer and she worked hard to prove her system, and eventually, teaming with the local Lions Club on Maui, was screening twenty-five schools across the island.

Chelsea's tenacity won over the locals; they now screen children on the four biggest islands. Her work there also led to an unexpected gift: CNN did a video feature on her in their 2015 *CNN Heroes* special.

CNN's spotlight on Half Helen caused the foundation's workload to explode, going from screening about 2,500 children a year to 9,000. Chelsea was delighted, but knew this massive surge would create logistical issues.

The admin involved in getting all the results from the screenings and contacting the parents of those children whose tests had indicated vision or hearing problems to give them recommendations was heavily labor-intensive and time-consuming. So Half Helen hired a software developer to build a time-saving app that allowed schools to upload the results from the test and email them to parents. "The first time we used it here in Austin, we cut the normal processing time from three to six months to two to three weeks!" Chelsea says. This huge labor-saving measure gives nurses much more time to focus on that small subset of children with serious vision problems and help them get access to care, one of Chelsea's goals.

. . .

I'M INSPIRED BY the remarkable work Chelsea and Half Helen have done, and I wondered what her vision for the foundation was.

Chelsea told me about her project to create a 44-foot mobile vision clinic complete with two onboard optometry offices. Known as *Optical Prime*, the mobile clinic will travel to schools and businesses, bringing care right to the patient. "I'm really excited about this part!" Chelsea exclaimed.

Half Helen's reach continues to expand. They have now screened more than 45,000 children between the ages of 4 and 18, and that number is growing fast. They expect to test 10,000 more in the 2019–2020 school year. But the statistic closest to Chelsea's heart? The Half Helen Foundation has helped more than 250 children avoid preventable blindness.

And while her foundation has helped many children, Chelsea recalls one moment in particular that showed her what a gift she was offering. Just after starting Half Helen, she was screening children at a health fair. A mother brought in her seven-year-old son, who had passed all the school vision tests, but was still having trouble seeing, and had fallen two grade levels behind in reading. Chelsea's magic camera showed that he was severely farsighted—able to see things at a distance and easily read an eye chart . . . but couldn't read a book held 10 inches away!

Chelsea sent him and his mother to the mobile vision care bus at the event, and in 45 minutes, the little boy stepped out, proudly wearing a brand-new pair of glasses. Hugging his mother, he looked into her face and beamed in amazement. "Mama! You have freckles! I didn't know that!"

A heartwarming moment confirming Chelsea was on the right path.

IF YOU'VE EVER HAD the urge to start a nonprofit like Half Helen, Chelsea has some advice: "Spend as much time as you can volunteering or interacting and learning about the cause you're passionate about. I jumped into the vision screening space without really doing the research to see who else was around me. I probably could have structured more effective partnerships or collaborations if I'd done my homework, but at twenty-three, I thought I knew everything. Don't reinvent the wheel. Learn your space, and find partners who are established."

TAKE ACTION

INSPIRED BY MY conversation with Chelsea, I went to an optometrist and had my eyes tested for the first time in about twenty years. I discovered that I have a mild prescription, and recently ordered a pair of glasses with a blue light filter to take the pressure off my eyes while staring at a screen all day. It was reassuring to know that my eyes were in great health. If you haven't had your vision screened in a while,

I'm sure you can guess what Chelsea would suggest . . . get your eyes tested!

If you are based in the United States, go to thinkaboutyoureyes.com, type in your ZIP code to find a local eye doctor, and make an appointment for an eye exam. If you have vision insurance, you can contact your provider to find a specialist covered by your plan. For those on a budget, search "free eye exams" or "low-cost eye exams" online to find organizations and nonprofits that provide affordable or free options near you. If you have children, visit halfhelen.org to see if the Half Helen Foundation provides free screenings in your area.

DR. ROLA HALLAM:

UNLEASHING YOUR INNER HUMANITARIAN

For anesthesiologist Rola Hallam, bad days were not uncommon. Big-city emergency rooms can be places of human suffering and misery, and her London hospital was no exception. Rola had helped many of her patients get through the worst days of their lives. And while often testing the limits of both her skills and her empathy, her job was rewarding enough to keep her going.

But then a terrible new dimension entered: war. In war, bad days are the rule, not the exception.

So when the worst day of Rola's own life began, it seemed like any other.

She was volunteering during her time off at a medical clinic near war-ravaged Aleppo in northwestern Syria, her home country. The work was routine: treating patients, inspecting supplies, and overseeing staff.

Then all hell broke loose.

It started when someone rushed in with a badly burned baby. While the staff was trying to understand what had caused the unusual burns, the clinic's doors burst open and in came a frenzied flood of victims, almost all children and teenagers.

Though Rola was a veteran physician, she had never seen anything like this. Covered in an odd white dust, the patients' clothing and skin hung off them. One child was walking with his arms stretched out like a zombie. The rest were either silenced by shock or wailing in agony. As Rola put it, the "heart-wrenching smell of burnt flesh" filled the hospital.

As she and her staff frantically scrambled to treat the wounded, they got word that it had been an aerial bomb, insidiously designed to incinerate everything in its path, dropped on a schoolyard filled with children waiting to be picked up. Now at least they had a clue as to how to treat all those barbarically injured children.

Amid the carnage, the victim most etched into her memory was a grotesquely burnt boy of about sixteen. Numbed by shock, all Rola could bring herself to ask him was, "How are you?"

Despite his grievous wounds, he tried to smile, but could only manage to whisper, "I'm okay," because his throat was so badly seared.

Rola knew his injured throat would soon swell, causing him to suffocate. She struggled to hold back her tears as she sedated him and put in a breathing tube so he would slip away gently, rather than suffocate to death. It broke her heart, but only strengthened her determination to help.

ROLA HALLAM likes to say she was born a doctor. Dreaming of being a doctor like her father, young Rola would perform "critical, life-saving" operations on her friends' Barbie and Sindy dolls. Early on, she developed a deep concern over the disparity between the haves and have-nots of the world. As much as she wanted to be a doctor, she was also convinced it wouldn't be enough: she wanted to truly help the poor and the forgotten.

When Rola was thirteen, her parents decided to move from Syria to the UK for professional reasons. She arrived in the country speaking no English. Two years later, still learning the language, she told her teachers she wanted to make her dream real and apply to medical school.

They didn't take her very seriously.

"They said my grades weren't good enough," she recalls. They felt she was overreaching, that she should stick to studying biology or chemistry at university rather than applying to medical school. "I thought it was the most ridiculous thing I'd ever heard! Of course I was going to at least try and give myself a chance."

Even at a young age, Rola's strength of character and determination were evident. Her teachers' words were an early lesson to her, not only in following your dream despite the doubts others may cast on it, but, perhaps even more so, on the importance of trying.

"Don't ever let someone stop you from doing something that you feel is your purpose in life," she told me emphatically.

It became clear during our interview that her work is inspired by the cruel inequities plaguing so many societies. As a child, Rolla's family lived relatively well because her parents were professionals, but she also saw how the rest of Syria lived, including her own extended family in the rural parts of the country. It was this contrast, so close to home, that sharpened her awareness of life's essential unfairness.

Even before she finished medical school, she was forging a different path than most young physicians, always asking for time off to travel the world to aid those in need. She volunteered as a charity trek doctor in the Himalayas, then as a flying doctor covering much of Africa. Later in her career, she sought to help build the capacity of healthcare organizations themselves, making them operate more efficiently—so they could do the most good for as many people as possible.

Then 2011 changed everything. Her beloved Syria—beset by the worst drought ever recorded, the influx of more than 1.5 million refugees from the Iraq War, and the cruelty of an oppressive regime—saw its citizens pushed to the brink.

Rola understood their feelings.

"No wonder the revolution happened. There were so many people who had had enough, and were asking for fairness, freedom, and human dignity because of this massive disparity between the 'haves' and 'have-nots.'"

That vast gulf of injustice, inflamed by almost two decades of iron-fisted control by the Assad regime, was finally
too much for the Syrians to bear. When they protested peace-
fully, their reasonable demands were met with swift and furious repression, which quickly spread across Syria.

Rola's country was suddenly in flames. But she is adamant about not calling this a civil war, as many media outlets
have done. "Correction: It is state-sponsored murder and
oppression," she says.

Like most people, I knew there was a war in Syria, but
until I met this amazing woman, I had no idea how utterly
horrific it was. Without qualification, it is one of the worst
humanitarian disasters of the twenty-first century. And unlike storms, earthquakes, or tsunamis, this disaster is entirely
man-made.

The Assad regime joined with Russia to squash the resistance. Governments slaughtering their own people is a
tragically familiar scenario, but this genocide has claimed
more than half a million lives and forced as many as twelve
million Syrians from their homes—in a country of less than
nineteen million! Usually, when such a humanitarian cata-
clysm occurs, large aid organizations enter the picture, but
the situation in Syria was so precarious, it scared off all but
the most tenacious.

Russian jets, under Assad's direction, have targeted not
just schools but hospitals, installing a sense of fear for everyone working in those critical facilities. Syria has become
a shattered hellscape.

It's also rife with personal tragedy for Rola. "By the second year," she tells me, "thirty members of my family had been killed, and many of their farms burned."

While others found the losses too painful to bear, Rola couldn't walk away. She'd never worked in an active war zone, but these were her people, and she had to do something. Her charity work had shown her she could make a difference, however small. Only now it wasn't some exotic foreign region that needed her help—it was the place where she was born.

"It's about heeding that internal call," she says matter-of-factly. "Many of us have it, but we suppress it for various reasons. It's just having the courage to say, 'No, this is what's right for me, right now.'"

Despite her full-time job in London, Rola began carefully planning her missions, sacrificing holidays to work with different Syrian organizations. She worked primarily with Hand in Hand for Syria, with whom she helped set up six hospitals in the northern part of the country. Along with supporting eighty field hospitals, the group operates the only pediatric hospital in the region.

Rola was also the subject of a riveting BBC *Panorama* documentary, *Saving Syria's Children*. One of her major frustrations is the lack of factual information being reported in the worldwide press about the Syrian crisis, so she was instrumental in getting the documentary made and the word out.

If you watch it, be warned—it is a powerful piece of reporting, but deeply disturbing. The terrible incident this story opens with occurred at the time of its production: brutally burned children; families on the brink of despair; one chaotic scene after another. But through Rola and the documentary, I also learned about some of the remarkable women and men risking their lives every day to help others.

People like Dr. Amina.

The stress of the conflict in Syria has caused a dramatic rise in premature births, but because many of the country's hospitals have been bombed, there are no facilities left to treat these mothers and babies. This didn't stop Dr. Amina. She delivered dozens of often sick and premature babies on her own kitchen floor. Rola was so moved by this unstoppable heroine that she worked with Hand in Hand for Syria to help Dr. Amina expand her home to include a delivery room and clinic.

In the documentary, we also see another unsung hero, an exhausted doctor *giving his own blood* to save a patient because his makeshift hospital had none to give.

And then Rola told me a story of extraordinary courage: that of Nurse Malaki.

"A pediatric nurse, she was literally bombed and nearly killed six times. She spent six months in the hospital with severe burns, and honestly, I thought she was going to die. And yet each time she was released, she went straight back to the children's hospital to carry on caring for small children."

Rola admits that most people would not have stayed long enough to see the first bomb fall, "let alone the second, third, fourth, fifth . . . and *sixth*, you know? Those people really renew my faith in humanity, and I would love everyone to know about them, be inspired by them."

Targeting hospitals and schools with bombs is monstrous, but in these horrific crises, there were sparkling rays of humanity. After the children's hospital was bombed, the staff wanted to rebuild, but had no money to do so. Rola decided to act. She appealed for donations, and in just twelve days, with thousands heeding the call from around the world, they raised an astounding £150,000. This was people power at its finest. She then led a convoy driving from London to the Syrian border with all the hospital provisions, so that the hospital could be rebuilt in a safe area. "The doctors and nurses were so moved by people's efforts that they call it Hope Hospital for Children," she said. The facility now treats up to five thousand children per month.

Rola, Nurse Malaki, the tenacious hospital personnel, and the generosity of those who donated to rebuild the hospital remind us of the good in humanity. Typically humble, Rola admits she never planned to be an advocate or speaker, doing TV interviews and TED Talks. She hadn't even planned to be the subject of the BBC documentary at first. But she realized that being a powerful witness to the inhumanity inside the Syrian war zone was one of the best ways to help those trapped within it. "When you're truly speaking from the heart, you can touch people, and people do help," she says.

During her missions, Rola also learned something that surprised, then angered her: "I used to think it was the big international organizations that go around saving the world. I now know different." While large international NGOs get the vast majority of the aid budget, these agencies are bureaucratic machines, and they're expensive to run. Rola was outraged at the injustice of funds going to administrative costs rather than to the people who really need it.

Millions of people were suffering and dying needlessly because the people who actually saved lives—the local doctors, nurses, and aid workers—were not getting the resources they needed to do their jobs. "It's about time we changed that," says Rola. "I realized that that was the situation everywhere in crisis, not just Syria."

Rola found a research paper by Local to Global Justice that highlighted how Syrian NGOs and charities were doing 75 percent of the humanitarian work in Syria but getting less than 1 percent of the available budget.

No wonder she was furious.

"If your community went up in flames, you'll be the one trying to put those flames out. Yet we were getting globally one percent of our aid budget, and that was when I thought, 'Right. We can do better than this.'" Rola subsequently founded CanDo, a nonprofit, crowd-funded social enterprise, to bring healthcare and human connection to the world's worst war-ravaged regions. The first line in CanDo's manifesto is: "We have the courage to imagine a better world, the resourcefulness to make it real, the humility to know we don't have all the answers, and the tenacity to stand up again after we have fallen."

"And that's the idea of the CanDo platform," Rola says. "Bringing together the global community with those able to provide those critical health and life-saving services. Finding trusted local humanitarians who are doing amazing work and supporting them."

Rola's rewriting of this age-old charitable donation system now gives the donor power over where their money goes, with comprehensive feedback and reporting on what their money is actually doing. Even better, it gives local care-givers direct access to badly needed funds that previously might have gone towards the running costs of big NGOs.

Rola likes to call it "people power."

DR. ROLA HALLAM is changing the rules about international healthcare charities and how they operate. CanDo is truly giving the power back to the people—donors, providers, and receivers. The notion of fully democratizing a charity is empowering for those who want to give but fear their money is not actually getting to the people who need it.

But far more needs to be done to make the best use of charitable funds. Rola says, "My vision is that we will be able to go to the various decision-makers and say 'Look, this works. You need to change the way you are working.' Because no matter how much CanDo is able to do, it's not going to be enough if the whole system doesn't change."

I love how she channeled her outrage to create a charity with no middlemen, and I also love her take on the word *humanitarian*: "Let's redefine 'humanitarian.' My definition is someone who cares about the welfare of other humans and is willing to act, from something so small as lending a hand when someone falls over or giving someone a fiver because they're hungry to bigger acts."

You might not be as devoted as Nurse Malaki, or the doctor donating his own blood, or even Rola herself, but you can be a humanitarian every day in the loving actions you take toward others.

Rola has seen too many terrors up close, but has words of hope for everyone: "It's really about unleashing your inner humanitarian. Realizing that we all absolutely have the responsibility and ability to positively impact other people's lives and create positive change in the world. So find your power."

TAKE ACTION

IF YOU'RE AS MOVED by Rola, her work, and the situation in Syria as I was, go to candoaction.org right now and make a donation, no matter how big or small, to help CanDo save lives in Syria.

CHAD BERNSTEIN:
THE MUSIC MAN

They thought it was going to be easy. A piece of cake. The musicians were excited to be presenting their skills to a group of young people. A friend of one of the band's members was working as a counselor at a detention center for troubled youth, and had mentioned a career day where members of the community came to the center and spoke to the teens about their jobs. Usually the speakers were bankers or lawyers, so he thought it would be interesting for the kids to meet some musicians and maybe even hear some music. "They need something cool to get their attention" was the pitch from the friend. "I can't seem to break through to them, and having somebody come in and talk about installing cable or something is just gonna lose 'em again."

The band, Suénalo, billed themselves as Afro-Latin funk. Its members, all in their early twenties and thirties, loved what they did, and were thrilled by the idea of sparking that same love in the youngsters.

The musicians had spent plenty of time on the road and were used to having their gear inspected at various venues. So as they got ready to pass through security at the front door of the detention center, they didn't think anything of it. Until the guard looked at the guitar cases and shook his head.

"Can't bring in the guitars. Sorry."

Chad Bernstein, the band's trombone player, gave the man a half smile. "They obviously need their instruments. You're kidding, right?"

The security guard's expression went from tired to irritated. "No guitars." Then, for graphic impact, he added, "The strings can be taken off and used to strangle you."

Strangle us? Chad thought, and wondered what they'd gotten themselves into.

Of all the gigs they'd ever played, in countries around the world, they'd never had someone warn them their own instruments might be used to kill them. This was a first. Despite the lethal warning, the band managed to talk the security guard into letting them keep their instruments, but just to be safe, he assigned two other guards to follow them. The musicians set up in a large room, and the kids—about forty of them— were brought in, their grim, even angry, young faces hardly receptive. It was another first for the artists: staring down a crowd that was hostile and utterly disinterested from the get-go.

Chad hoped mentioning that he'd played with Shakira and Pitbull might stir interest.

It didn't.

The artists, now a little thrown, tried talking about the career of a musician, from touring to copyright to the business aspects, assuming the mechanics of making money might get some interest.

Nada. Crickets.

Sensing that they couldn't win, the band decided to play one song and get out. They began playing and their MC started rapping, and for the first time the kids seemed to respond, their heads nodding to the beat.

Then something changed the entire dynamic.

One of the kids sang a lyric. A guard told him to "shut up and quit being disrespectful." But the musicians had heard something they liked and insisted, "No, no, please, sing that again."

The kid repeated the lyric, and the band sang it back. Then, one by one, the musicians began picking up the beat. The MC started freestyling a rap, going back and forth with the kid, and in no time, other kids jumped in. Suddenly the band and the kids were creating a song from scratch. This spontaneous jam session, with a bunch of kids who had appeared totally disconnected just moments before, highlighted a very important point: music has the power to unite everyone. Chad, his bandmates, and the kids were all in musical heaven, and the energy in the room was electric.

After they wrapped up the song, the previously unreachable audience was suddenly fascinated by the band, asking, "What was that?" and "How did you know what to play?" In turn, the musicians had questions for them, like, "Who do you like to listen to? Who's your favorite rapper?" They then moved on to deeper questions, like what the kids had done to land in the detention center; how they felt about it, and how they felt about the system. Music had opened the doors for the kids to let go and talk authentically about what was going on in their lives.

For Chad, that moment crystallized an idea that had been germinating in his head for years. "As a professional musician, the disappearance of music in schools concerned me a lot, because I would have been lost without music," Chad says. He had noticed the need for a long time, but not known how to respond. Now he had the beginnings of an answer, one that would change the lives of so many kids like those in the juvenile detention center that day.

CHAD BERNSTEIN comes from people who, despite their humble means, blazed their own paths and broke away from the pack. His grandfather was a child of the Depression and a third-grade dropout, but he worked hard and did everything he could to support his five kids. He was adamant that all his children get an education, and when he died of an unexpected heart attack at age fifty-two, Chad's father created a memorial scholarship fund in his father's honor, which helped put all five siblings through college, with money left over in the fund once they'd all graduated.

Chad's father received a degree from the prestigious Wharton School, the University of Pennsylvania's business school. His mother had graduated from high school two years early, at sixteen. The pair met in a training program at IBM. Very independent thinkers, they decided to raise Chad and his brother with a strong work ethic, emphasizing that you must earn what you have, and work as hard as necessary to achieve it.

As a kid, Chad was also surrounded by music and a love of art. He learned the Motown catalog driving around with his mother. The family moved to Chicago when Chad was in the fifth grade. He took that as an opportunity to reinvent himself, as he had begun to drift away from the principles his family had worked to instill in him. His love of music offered a natural direction, so he threw himself into it, eventually mastering a number of instruments, from keyboards to percussion to his first love, trombone.

When Chad was thirteen, his father insisted that he make a huge life choice. "The two things you love in life are music and sports," he said. "You've got to pick one and find your passion. Be the best at it, have that drive to excel, rather than compromising who you are to be something else."

This was a watershed moment for Chad. He remembers it as vividly as if it had happened yesterday. Chad chose music and went to work, entering every musical competition he could, especially where he could demonstrate his trombone skills.

• • •

CHAD'S FATHER had become an investor in emerging markets and traveled a lot for work. He took Chad on those trips when he could, giving his son a glimpse at the world outside of Chicago.

One day when Chad was with his father in Soweto, a township in South Africa, he shared his headphones with a local kid who came out of a tin-roofed shack to meet him. The kid's eyes lit up with joy when he heard the music by U2 that Chad was listening to, and it was then that Chad began to grasp the universal power of music. The more he traveled, the more he saw it. And those trips also instilled a deep love of world music in him.

Back home in Chicago, the young trombone virtuoso went to local clubs to find older, more experienced jazz musicians to jam with, and they were all impressed by this kid with the skills of an old pro. One group Chad connected with was "this old Polish dude that played the accordion and had a ten-piece ballroom band." Chad toured the Midwest with the band playing casinos and giving the older crowd the fox-trots and cha-chas they loved from days past. Despite being underage, Chad played in bars, something most mothers would be horrified by. But his own mother, who defied convention, encouraged him, because he was getting experience you could neither buy nor learn from a book.

While other kids were still practicing their scales, Chad held his own with his older bandmates. His constant immersion in playing everywhere from school to clubs, always honing his skills, gave him enormous experience at an early age, which underscores author Malcolm Gladwell's rule that it takes *10,000 hours* to master a skill or become a success in any field. But this massive gulf in experience between him and his peers led to a showdown with his mentor and high school band director, James Warrick.

The school had four levels of jazz band, and Chad, even as a freshman, felt he was easily operating at the highest level, Jazz One. The group would be taking a special trip to China the following year, and Chad assumed his spot was guaranteed.

At the end of his freshman year, Chad went to Mr. Warrick for his review and asked where he'd be placed the following year, already assuming he'd be in Jazz One. Instead, his mentor threw him for a loop. "Musically, you're totally ready for this," began Mr. Warrick. "But in terms of your attitude and professionalism, and mainly your arrogance, I'm not going to put you there."

Chad was stunned. But Mr. Warrick continued the assault on his ego: "Until you recognize the value in bringing other people up to your level instead of phoning it in because you think you're better than them, you're staying where you are."

Chad walked out of the meeting in a state of shock. While he hadn't intended to come across as arrogant, clearly he had. He was devastated that his apparently unbearable attitude, not his musical ability, would be his ruin. He realized that by not helping others get to his level, he wasn't being a team player, and that was what being in a band was all about—team play.

"It was a huge life lesson for me," Chad says. Rather than push against the criticism, he simply changed the way he operated and vowed to do better. He'd never thought of himself as a leader before, but he resolved right then and there to do a one-eighty, not just being a better band member but a better *leader*.

Over that summer, he spent a lot of time working on himself, musically and as a person. He embraced his leadership role—and ended up going to China with the advanced band during his sophomore year after all.

Chad went on to attend college on a music scholarship, and built a colorful career afterward, playing with people like the aforementioned Pitbull and Shakira, as well as will.i.am, Natalie Cole, Chaka Khan, John Legend, Phil Ramone, and many more.

But it was that incident at the detention center that stuck with him. Soon, that seed of an idea grew into Guitars Over Guns, an organization that pairs at-risk middle-schoolers with professional musicians as mentors to help them overcome hardship. This guidance gives the kids a way to find their creative voices and reach their potential as tomorrow's leaders. Acting as both music teachers and life coaches, Guitars Over Guns counselors provide young people with the kind of hands-on, caring attention that few of them have ever experienced.

Chad felt that society was "creating limitations the kids are living down to." With little expected of them, many would not try to rise above the low expectations. Having witnessed the instant explosion of attention in the room with the kids at the detention center, Chad knew he was on the right track.

Beginning as "a volunteer thing," Chad and his father, Bob, self-funded Guitars Over Guns and used the money left over in his grandfather's memorial scholarship fund to grow the program, and it soon evolved into a more formal structure. Bob not only helped incorporate the nonprofit, but chaired its board of directors as well. Chad brought in musicians who had the same sense of commitment as he did to act as mentors and teachers.

The first year of the program saw lines of trust gradually drawn between the kids and the musicians. It was, of course, a challenge to reach some of the students, whose lives had taught them to be wary of adults. But by the second year, as those relationships deepened, the kids began to rely on their mentors more, and the work took on a meaning beyond music.

The students started to share some of their personal stories and what they were going through, only to discover that the musicians, with their own long histories, were a lot more like them than they had imagined. The kids dropped their tough fronts and shared personal stories with each other, from family tragedies to ordinary struggles at school with friends. It was the start of many breakthroughs. Chad now considers some of the kids family, inviting them over for holidays or to play with his young children.

Chad describes his work with Guitars Over Guns as enormously satisfying. It showed him that even with a rewarding career in music doing what he loved, he could still do more and have more impact. So far the program has altered the lives of over 2,700 students, like Joshua and Sam.

JOSHUA WAS A BIG KID, very popular, with an easygoing attitude, who never seemed to take anything seriously. He would always show up to Guitars Over Guns sessions ten minutes late, and never seemed able to focus on a particular instrument, jumping from one to the next. But he showed up—however late—so the people running the program cut him some slack. His mentors discovered that despite Joshua's apparent confidence, he was very insecure, and his disruptive behavior only sought to cover this secret. They later found out he had some serious trauma at home, which likely compounded his feelings of insecurity.

Unfortunately, there was a limit. While Joshua showed talent, Chad finally had to sit him down and tell him he needed to straighten up and focus, partly because he was stealing attention from other kids who were taking the program seriously. He was asked to leave five times, but each time, he talked his way back into the program.

Though not prepared to play at the Guitars Over Guns graduation concert, Joshua showed up, looking a little sheepish. He surprised his mentors by asking if he could speak. Very eloquently, he confessed to the audience that he'd made it difficult for those running the program, but they still took a chance on him. He apologized for his behavior, and thanked the program and the mentors for not giving up on him. With tears in his eyes, he admitted that he didn't deserve to graduate from the program, but he wanted them to know how much it meant to him.

Chad and his fellow instructors were humbled. It was such a powerful gesture, from a kid they thought couldn't have cared less. It served as a lesson for everyone running Guitars Over Guns, who realized in that moment that "our job was not to judge whether the kids cared or not, but rather do what we do and let the kids decide."

CHAD SAYS THE KEY to building trust with young people is consistency. You have to show up and let them know you're committed. For the kids participating in Guitars Over Guns, many of the adults in their lives had done just the opposite, so they were understandably wary. They test the mentors, push their buttons to see what they are made of. The kids needed to see early on if the mentors held up, because if they didn't, they weren't going to waste their time . . . or risk having their hearts broken.

One of the best examples was a young girl who had built up a wall to protect her heart. Her name was Sam.

Sam was a tough kid. You didn't cross her. Taken from her mother by the state as a baby, she was adopted by her aunt, who raised her as her own daughter.

At school, Sam wasn't just a handful—she was a self-proclaimed terror. She fought constantly, got bad grades, skipped class, and was disrespectful, all to fit in with her peers—not realizing she was jeopardizing her future. Her behavior was so bad that one day, her aunt got a call from the principal saying that Sam would not be allowed back at school until the following year.

That same day, her aunt transferred her to another school. But Sam's behavior at her new school threatened to derail her there, too.

Then one day, on her way to detention, she noticed a Guitars Over Guns group in a classroom. Curious, she walked in and discovered another world. The kids in that room were dancing, singing, playing instruments, and creating art—they were having fun and Sam was intrigued. She ditched detention that day and never left Guitars Over Guns. Her aunt, hoping to inspire some creative energy in Sam, who she knew had smarts and talent and an interest in music, had previously bought her niece a used guitar. She learned to play the guitar quickly, and discovered a natural gift for singing.

After a year in the program, Sam had her first performance, at a venue called the Iron Inside. Petrified, she took the stage with her guitar in her hands. Chad, taking it all in from the side of the stage, could see her hands shaking as she grabbed the microphone. But when she began to sing, he watched her shoulders drop and her eyes close as she found her groove. When she finished, the room erupted in a big standing ovation, radiating love and joy.

When Sam came offstage, she was crying. Chad gave her a huge hug, congratulated her, and asked what she was crying about—she'd done such a great job. She replied, "I feel like I've been seen for the first time in my life. Like I was finally seen for who I am."

Sam went on to become an important member of the program, and from failing high school to graduating with honors. In her four years in Guitars Over Guns, she learned to love and accept herself. When she takes the stage now, as a young woman, she has the air of a poised, confident artist.

THIS IS THE HUMAN LEGACY that goes beyond anything Chad Bernstein hoped or expected when he created Guitars Over Guns.

It more than makes up for the early frustrations and growing pains of getting the program started and for the initial terror he felt when Suénalo walked into that detention center to face all those angry glares years before. After that jam session, Chad was inspired, and knew that as a musician, he had the ability to reach kids and change their lives. I'm so glad he trusted his intuition, took a leap of faith, and started something. His story is a reminder that if you feel called to do something that benefits others, to listen to that voice.

The world is facing a lot of issues. Sometimes it can be overwhelming, and you may wonder what you can do to help or if what you do can ever be enough. But Chad told me something that really resonated: "Sometimes I'd feel helpless, like what I was doing wasn't enough, but I had to remind myself that every tidal wave is made up of thousands of drops of water, and knowing that you matter, as one of those drops of water, you can make a difference."

TAKE ACTION

THIS IS SOMETHING Chad has his students in the Guitars Over Guns program do:

1. Write down one thing that you are not sure you can do, but want to do.

   _____

   _____

   _____

2. Commit to working toward it consistently for ten weeks.

3. Work toward this goal with someone, either a partner or a friend, and hold each other accountable. If you can't find someone, tell us on Instagram, @ionebutler and @upliftingcontent. Tag us in your posts or stories and keep us updated with your progress—we will hold you accountable!

PART 4

GAME-CHANGERS

Don't just play the game. Change it for good.
—Unknown

There are lots of different ways to define *game-changer*. In the Merriam-Webster dictionary, it is defined as "a newly introduced element or factor that changes an existing situation or activity in a significant way." The business dictionary definition is "a person or idea that transforms the accepted rules, processes, strategies and management of business functions."

My definition, for purposes of this chapter, is "a person who is willing to defy the status quo, question the way things are done, and find a better way." Now, it's not always easy to go against the grain. In the sixteenth and seventeenth centuries, the common consensus was that Earth was at the center of the universe, and the sun and stars revolved around it. We (of course) now know that not to be the case. But when Polish astronomer Nicolaus Copernicus dared to speak up about his game-changing (and unholy) theory that the earth circled the sun, he was condemned by the Catholic Church. Galileo suffered a similar fate for agreeing with Copernicus. And in between, Giordano Bruno, an astronomer and Dominican friar, received the harshest punishment for agreeing with Copernicus' explanation of the nature of our solar system by being burned at the stake.

It's a common theme throughout history. The Beatles and Elvis were told early on that their music was too loud and their behavior off-putting, and that they would never succeed. An agent told a young Arnold Schwarzenegger that he was "too big, no one could understand him, and no one could pronounce his name"—not long after that, Schwarzenegger became the world's largest box office star (not to mention later becoming the "Governator" of California). The founders of Airbnb were laughed out of investor meetings, or completely ignored, because no one could imagine people letting strangers from the internet rent a room in their home. The company's value is now estimated at a staggering $38 billion. Wasn't such a silly idea, was it?

It can be a lonely and scary journey for a game-changer. But just think of the positive impact you could make in the lives of others, and for our planet. In this chapter, you'll meet Maria Rose Belding, a young woman who was frustrated with the amount of food wasted in grocery stores and restaurants and the shortage of food in food banks—so she created a database to make the process of finding and distributing food to those in need far more efficient. Destiny Watford, a teen activist from one of the most polluted cities in America, confronted a huge corporation and refused to let a toxic trash incinerator be built in her community. Korin Sutton had an epiphany about human health and animal welfare after returning from deployment in Iraq, and became a vegan personal trainer who helps clients achieve remarkable health benefits by changing their lifestyle habits.

The truth is, anyone can be a game-changer. Do you have a big idea? Or even a small one no one else has considered? Are you ready to shake up your life, and possibly the world as well? If you answered yes to any of the above, I hope these stories will give you the courage to take the leap.

DESTINY WATFORD:
THE POWER OF DESTINY

"The most polluted place in America." Not exactly a great endorsement for any community, but in the neighborhood where Destiny Watford grew up, it was the truth. Curtis Bay is about sixty square blocks of low-income homes in South Baltimore, surrounded by one of the busiest industrial waterfronts in America. It's also one of the dirtiest neighborhoods in the country, with staggering pollution levels.

Curtis Bay has been a dumping ground for Maryland since the mid-nineteenth century, when it was established as a quarantine center for ships arriving from overseas. Like a grotesque environmental Berlin Wall, a fence divides the neighborhood where humans live and breathe from the deadly side, the area given over to huge, gross polluters. But before the factories took over completely, the industrial side was once a thriving community called Fairfield. The community's residents experienced high rates of birth deformities and lung cancer. Former Fairfield residents would describe riding a bike through the neighborhood and reaching a point where they couldn't breathe, as if they'd somehow been transported to another planet with an atmosphere of poison gas, not air. Even more horrific were the constant explosions from the chemical plants that sounded like bombs going off. Some likened living in Fairfield to being in an active combat war zone. "It was awful," Destiny observed. Sadly, the onslaught of industrialization created such health consequences for its residents that it became too much to bear (and survive), and the last family moved out in the 1990s.

When Destiny was sixteen, she discovered a terrifying plan to pump even more pollution, staggering levels of lead and mercury, into the atmosphere of her town. Even more horrifying was that the source of these deadly toxins was going to be built right next to her school! This discovery led Destiny to take the greatest stand of her young life, challenging the status quo and changing others' beliefs of what is possible for a teenager to accomplish.

DESTINY WATFORD had a very strict upbringing and spent a lot of her time in solitude, reading. This gave her plenty of time to reflect on what makes something right or wrong, as well as the concepts of justice and integrity. While she is a very different person now than she was then, what connects her to her younger self are her ideals about how the world should be and how people should treat each other. She also had far more trust in institutions when she was younger—and when facts about their motivations came to light and that trust was broken, she felt betrayed.

If you were to walk down the street in Curtis Bay back when Destiny was growing up, you'd have noticed a few things. First, the trucks. They were big, and there were a lot of them. Literally forty to eighty trucks *an hour* thundered down the small streets of Curtis Bay, their massive weight and earthquake-like rumbling shaking many of the town's homes so badly, their walls were literally cracking. Most of those poor and forgotten renters and homeowners could not afford to repair the damage, so they had to just sit back and watch as their homes crumbled.

Once you got past the trucks, you'd notice the coal. A lot of coal. It was accepted as normal for children to play in the shadows of mountains of the stuff. "Oh, okay, it's just a black mountain of coal. Move on," is how Destiny explains this acceptance. For years, the coal dust would blow into the homes of Curtis Bay's residents, covering everything as if they lived near an eternally erupting volcano. People would put their laundry out to dry, and the next day it would be completely covered in coal dust. And the behemoth factories and refineries continue to spout toxic smoke.

Destiny could literally see the poisonous fumes in the air, which often smelled like rotten eggs. It riled her beloved grandmother's chronic respiratory problems so much that the poor woman had a hard time just catching her breath.

Destiny grew up hearing jokes about the lingering chemical stench, accepted as the unalterable fate of the neighborhood. Local politicians weren't inclined to help, because they needed to protect the corporations whose factories surrounded the community. In high school, Destiny and her friends tried to be philosophical about the pollution: it was just part of the landscape, like the steep hills lined with rundown row houses and the stark industrial wasteland hugging the bay. "You almost forget that it's there," she told me. "You know it's present; you can see it, smell it, hear it, but it's something you learn to live with."

One day, on her way to school, seventeen-year-old Destiny noticed an abandoned medical facility on the banks of the Patapsco River, which opens to form Baltimore's waterfront. She had walked past the derelict building nearly every day for years, but that day something looked different. On a sun-bleached sign on the chain link fence surrounding the property, she could barely make out the words "Energy Answers." She didn't think much of it at the time, and kept walking.

Several weeks later, Destiny went on a school trip to the theater to see *An Enemy of the People*, a play written in 1882 by Henrik Ibsen. It's the story of a small town that becomes corrupt when greed is allowed to triumph over the health of its citizens. In the play, it's discovered that the town's public baths have become dangerously polluted, but shutting them down could lead to economic chaos. Keeping it quiet would not upset the prosperity of the richer citizens, but it would expose more people to the toxins.

Ibsen's nearly century-and-a-half-old play resonated with Destiny. Its explosive premise eerily echoed her own situation. She also divined Ibsen's deeper message: that bad things persist because truth has a life cycle, and if not actively promoted, it dies out. She saw, too, that the people in Ibsen's play had a binary choice: live in poverty but have clean water in the baths, or have money and resources but be poisoned.

Destiny's social conscience was awakened that day. And, as it turns out, the timing of this awakening was fortuitous. Soon after, she heard about a proposal to allow even more pollution in Curtis Bay. She began to do some research, and discovered an alarming but perhaps unsurprising study published by MIT researchers in 2013, that found that more people died from pollution-linked causes in Baltimore than any other city in America. The study noted that 113 out of every 100,000 Maryland residents were likely to die from long-term exposure to pollution in a given year. And she already knew Curtis Bay took the brunt of that foul credit.

Apparently, it was about to get worse.

According to newspaper accounts, Energy Answers Int'l. donated $100,000 to the national Democratic Governors Association, then chaired by Maryland Governor Martin O'Malley. The check was made out on the same day he announced his intention to sign a bill that would categorize garbage incineration as a renewable energy source, putting it on the same footing as wind or solar providers, a change that was potentially worth millions to Energy Answers. Despite appearances to the contrary, the Governor denied that his decision was influenced by the company's donation to the DGA.

Energy Answers was planning to build a giant trash incinerator on the site of that abandoned medical facility Destiny walked by every day, and construction was set to soon begin. Alarmed, Destiny did more research, and discovered that the planned incinerator would be the largest ever built on United States soil.

The project's supporters claimed it would provide power for Destiny's own high school and create more jobs for locals; based on those promises, the neighborhood did not oppose the incinerator. But like it was in Ibsen's play, the truth was being concealed from public view. Unless you dug for it. Like Destiny. Heavy metals would be pumped into the atmosphere by that incinerator each year, further condemning the residents of Curtis Bay. And in a sickening twist, because the incinerator was now designated a renewable energy source, state law prohibitions against locating the incinerator near schools was waived. Destiny couldn't believe what she was reading. She was angry, and she was motivated. It really infuriated her when she read about Energy Answers's big donation to the DGA. It was pretty easy for her to connect the dots on who was scratching who's back. "Being woke means beginning to question things. Recognizing that the things you thought were normal are not normal, they are obscene, they are injustice, they should not exist," Destiny explains.

She decided enough was enough. Yes, she was just a high school student in a poor neighborhood, but she knew that movements didn't require money or status so much as belief and tenacity. Gandhi and Martin Luther King Jr. weren't millionaires with influence or YouTube stars with huge audiences; they were simply brave men who saw injustice and spoke up about it—inspiring others to join them in turn. It was time for Destiny to speak up.

She had always been a good student who knew her facts, but she was also shy. She understood that becoming an activist would require her to get out of her comfort zone and face the public. But because there was so much at stake, she gathered her courage and took action.

She reached out to friends and classmates, got them on board, and formed the advocacy group Free Your Voice. They made it their mission to educate the residents of Curtis Bay about the history of pollution in Baltimore. At first the response was predictable—they were just kids, they were misinformed, how could they think they knew more than the government or corporations? They listened politely to the critics but kept going, undaunted, knowing that they were in the right. Destiny told me about the time she went to speak at a senior citizens center. As Destiny began explaining how dangerous the incinerator would be for the community, an elderly woman interrupted her presentation. "Excuse me, young lady," she announced. "But we love the incinerator." The older resident's statement started a mini revolt with others in the group who all chimed in about how great Energy Answers was, providing jobs and doing things for the community like donating money for a park bench.

Destiny was stunned and couldn't believe that people were gullible enough to believe Energy Answers's blatant propaganda, causing them to support something so destructive; it was literally a threat to their lives. Destiny left the meeting in shock, her tail between her legs. When she shared this story with me, she laughed hysterically at how awkward it was and how naive she had been at the time, but it did teach her to be more prepared for future meetings. The next time, she told me, she returned armed with evidence, facts, and information for those who thought this deadly incinerator was a great idea.

One thing the locals *did* know was that for decades, they had been pushed and squeezed out of their communities by industrialization. What could have been valuable waterfront property was defiled and ravaged by big business. Destiny warned people that Curtis Bay might not survive much longer if they allowed the power brokers to shove them any further. Just because that had been Curtis Bay's past, she implored them, didn't mean it had to be the neighborhood's future.

Destiny led her army of activists by example, knocking on doors, telling the story over and over, warning of the dangers, and eventually even convincing older people like her grandmother's friends to sign petitions against the incinerator. They managed to get two thousand people in that small community to send testimonials about their health to the Maryland Energy Administration, as well as post them on social media. The movement caught fire, and went viral. Destiny soon captured the attention of local government, and was asked to speak before the Baltimore City Public School board.

She had originally only been allocated a couple of minutes to speak but the presentation turned into a twenty-minute "event." The room was filled with students, teachers, and parents from across the city packed in like sardines. They'd made art, parents and students spoke about why the board should not support the incinerator, and two members of Destiny's group stood inches away from the board as they performed a song about incineration and what it was like growing up in Curtis Bay. At the end they received a standing ovation from the board.

The response was explosive, channeling the community's outrage and causing the mayor and the district's representative in Congress to withdraw their support for the incinerator.

Feeling the momentum, Destiny and her group formed the Community Land Trust, an organization designed to give Curtis Bay's residents the power to protect themselves from such predatory exploitation. Their plan was to go to potential customers of Energy Answers—schools, libraries, even the city—and argue that the company they had hoped would bring them cheap energy was doing so but at a terrible cost. And it wasn't just going to be damaging to Destiny's small community, but Baltimore in general and really a large part of Maryland, too. With their new, louder voice they stalled construction by convincing all twenty-two of Energy Answers's slated customers to back out of their contracts.

But their victory was only temporary.

Their campaign had succeeded in scaring off Energy Answers's potential customers, but despite that blow to its bottom line their enormous adversary was still standing. Even though Energy Answers's building permits had expired in December 2015, the Maryland Department of the Environment (MDE), whose job it was to protect citizens from pollution, had not officially acknowledged that the permits had expired.

Even after spoiling the deals with all their users, Destiny and her team were shocked to discover that Energy Answers was still planning to go ahead and begin construction in January 2016.

Dismayed but still standing their ground, the group upped their attack by taking video testimonials from those who would be negatively impacted by the poisonous billion-dollar incinerator and sent the MDE letters from lawyers, environmentalists, and doctors outlining all the reasons why the facility should not be supported economically, environmentally, and morally, expecting them to uphold the law and stop Energy Answers from building with expired permits.

The MDE's response? Silence.

Yet Destiny and her team were not to be underestimated, understanding full well what those in politics call "optics."

"This was around the time that Freddie Gray was murdered and the riots were happening," Destiny said. "So there's this huge, ugly spotlight on Baltimore and how we deal with injustice and it's not acceptable to the public for a government organization's response to be silence."

The activists then held a rally of over 200 people to deliver their sunflower petitions (the sign of their campaign because the sunflower absorbs toxins) to the reception desk of the MDE asking them to uphold the law. The response? This time the MDE locked the doors and ignored the protestors. The underhanded move really riled the residents of Curtis Bay. They channeled their fury and created such a public relations ruckus they finally managed to get a delegation of nine into a meeting with Ben Grumbles, the Secretary of the Environment.

They blindsided Grumbles by staging a sit-in resulting in seven of them being arrested for civil obedience. "People sacrificed their freedom for this movement. It was a very clear message that we were not going away." Brilliantly grasping the power of persistence, Destiny continued, "We were just constantly bombarding MDE every day after that."

Finally in March of 2016, the MDE upheld the law and announced that due to "lack of continuous construction" the building permit for the Energy Answers's incinerator was "invalid." It was the coup de grâce Destiny had been praying for. The titan had toppled. "The incinerator was defeated and I remember screaming and being really excited. It was really awesome."

Destiny and her friends had gone up against an industrial giant and had come away triumphant. But there was one more honor Destiny never expected. Every year, the Goldman Environmental Foundation awards a prize to one grassroots environmental activist from each of the world's six inhabited continental regions: Africa, Asia, Europe, Islands & Island Nations, North America, and South & Central America. The prize is often referred to as the "Green Nobel," and the 2016 North American recipient had never even heard of it when she received the announcement at her home in Curtis Bay, Maryland. "At first, I thought somebody was pulling my leg," she says, smiling.

Destiny gratefully accepted the award, but in her characteristically humble manner credited the achievement to all the people who had fought alongside her—virtually her entire community.

The fight for a just cause often begins with one voice, and in this case, it was Destiny's. At first, the odds seemed stacked against her, but she felt she had no other choice. She won her fight, and the world—and particularly Curtis Bay—is a better place because of her.

Destiny graduated from college with a degree in journalism. She believes her life's work is to make sure voices that matter get heard.

TAKE ACTION

DESTINY IS MOST PROUD of the work she has done with fellow community members, bringing people together and allowing others to feel safe to open up and talk about their concerns and be active in their communities.

If Destiny's story inspired you, find a cause you feel passionate about close to home and get involved with a local community effort. Is there something that bothers you in your community? Does something need to be cleaned up or fixed? Are there any dangers in your community that have been ignored? Find a cause and do something about it. Perhaps you could join your child's PTA or become a more active member. Attend a local city or town council meeting; get involved in your local government and be part of the discussion. Be an active citizen and contribute to democracy. Like Destiny, you too have the power to make a huge positive impact.

MARIA ROSE BELDING:
FEED THE BODY,
FEED THE SOUL

It's easy to be impressed with Maria Rose Belding. In her short twenty-three years, she has accomplished and given so much. It was hard finding time to schedule our interview, because she has a lot going on. As a pre-med college senior who also happens to head a massive nonprofit, she should be intimidating, but instead, her open, bubbly, and warm demeanor immediately makes you feel like you've known her forever. She has an easy sense of humor backed by a razor-sharp intellect and the timing of a stand-up comedian, so it's no surprise that she is a trailblazer and the founder of a database helping to solve two of America's serious problems simultaneously: reducing food waste and feeding the hungry.

Growing up in the small town of Pella, Iowa, a very old Dutch community, Maria Rose sometimes felt out of place.

Her family was Sicilian and Black Irish, as evinced by her jet-black hair. Attitudes in Pella could be provincial, and Maria Rose caught the brunt of it.

"The community was so white that my family and I were kind of cast in the role of 'people of color,' even though by almost all definitions, we're not. So it was really isolating. The literal motto of the town is 'If you ain't Dutch, you ain't much.'"

This sentiment bubbled up one day as she and her brother played together. "Some lady called the school to warn them that there were Mexicans on the playground. Not even that we were doing something, just literally, 'There are Mexicans on the playground.'"

The xenophobia was confusing for a child, and as early as five years old, Maria Rose found solace in her church, helping others. "I grew up volunteering in the food pantry. That's kind of where my whole ethos came from. Peace Lutheran Church in Pella, Iowa. Lots of cows, not a lot of people."

She also cites as a strong influence her mother, who encouraged Maria Rose to see all others as equals. A middle school teacher, her mom created a class called Pure PE, where kids with social, emotional, and physical disabilities were paired with developmentally average kids. Each child had to adapt for their partner. "We would play dodgeball, and one of my partners, Caleb, was in a motorized wheelchair," Maria Rose remembers. "So he would steer, and I would ride on the back of his chair and throw the dodgeballs, and duck behind him while he covered me."

She learned quite a bit in Pure PE about walking in the other person's shoes.

From the time she was five or six, Maria Rose dreamed of being a doctor to help people be healthy. As a type 1 diabetic ("My pancreas is dead. I don't make any insulin."), she was exquisitely aware of the necessity of healthy eating, so she was surprised when she learned so many of the folks who came to the food pantry had type 2 diabetes, with worse blood sugar numbers than her own. She knew it was because they weren't getting the proper nutrition and her food pantry—with only shelf-stable goods available—wasn't helping.

Growing up in a small town also presented other obstacles.

"I am queer. I am bi, but they thought I was a lesbian, and they were very, very, very conservative, so I hid a lot because in the pantry, nobody hit me in there. The pantry was a safe place, but it was also a place where I was learning a lot and realized I could find value."

This was where she discovered another strong female role model: Melissa.

"Melissa ran the pantry and runs it still. She's an actual angel. I saw how far she was willing to go, and how hard she worked, to try to get more healthy food," Maria Rose says. Despite her youth, she immediately saw the holes in the food pantry system. "It was very clear to me that this was not a Melissa problem, not a management issue. This is a systems issue—she didn't have the tools that she needed."

Maria Rose felt there had to be a better way, but wasn't sure what that was.

As she got older, her commitment to the pantry never changed, but her understanding of how things worked did. By fourteen, she had realized that different food pantries weren't communicating with each other. Worse, she saw restaurants, grocery stores, and other outlets simply throwing away so much food, while food pantries and soup kitchens were dealing with both a lack of food and disorganization. It was frustrating for her, knowing that the grocery store was "like a mile, tops, from the church, and they would throw away fruit. But we couldn't communicate with them to get the fruit."

By then, she also knew it was hardly just a local problem: approximately forty million people in America face hunger, and consumers and businesses waste up to 40 percent of the country's food supply each year.

It seemed like madness.

The situation that perfectly distilled the problem was what Maria Rose amusingly refers to as the "Kraft Dinosaur."

"So this local church decided they were going to give our food pantry ten thousand boxes of macaroni and cheese for Christmas. Nice, except it's so many more boxes of mac and cheese than people within fifty miles [can use]. We were struggling to get it out to the clients, because number one, human beings can only eat so much mac and cheese, and number two, the least expensive part of macaroni and cheese is the box. You need the milk and the butter at home."

Maria Rose watched Melissa frantically phoning and

faxing other local food pantries, trying to find a home for some of the boxes, but getting mostly disconnected numbers and faxes that went nowhere. Frustrated, Melissa threw her family and a portion of the Kraft Dinosaur in her car and delivered it to a pantry in Michigan. That's when Maria Rose had an aha moment.

Her premise seemed absurdly simple: "Why are we not using the internet?"

Maria Rose was excited to share her idea with Melissa, but she wasn't sure how it would be received. "Teenage girls are very used to being told that our thoughts or our likes or our concerns are not legitimate," she told me. She and Melissa went for coffee, and Maria Rose laid out what she saw as the problem and how she visualized fixing it.

"She took me to get my very first latte and listened to this idea that I had. And I will never forget how she listened to me, how she treated my ideas and my thoughts as legitimate. And to have this person who is an expert, or the closest I was going to get to an expert on the national food pantry scene, listening to me and telling me what she thought was extraordinary."

Melissa's response was clear and direct: "This makes sense. I think you should build this. Make sure it's free."

And, so inspired, Maria Rose did.

SHE CALLED HER brainchild MEANS, for Matching Excess and Need for Stability (because "a fourteen-year-old me had a fondness for acronyms"), and with it, she was ready to change the world. Except it didn't happen as quickly as she wanted. A typical kid who knew her way around a phone and a computer, she didn't have the technical expertise to make MEANS a fully functioning clearinghouse for matching food needs with food sources. Still, she worked on the project throughout high school, searching for technical solutions.

At eighteen years old, as she was starting college, she knew she needed help for MEANS to fully blossom. Luckily, a friend introduced Maria Rose to her brother, Grant Nelson, a pre-law student and self-taught programmer. Their first meeting started rather inauspiciously, when Grant forgot she was coming, got home late, and found that Maria Rose had been waiting on his doorstep for four hours. He apologized profusely, but his patient guest was far more interested in his reaction to her idea than his apologies.

The verdict? "Grant loved it."

As it turned out, Grant also had a "start-up mentality," which helped enormously, and he became the cofounder. They officially launched the MEANS database to the world in March 2015.

It took off immediately.

No one had ever thought of connecting the massive number of food pantries and soup kitchens with all those sources of excess food. As Maria Rose recalls, "We started raising money. We won the George Washington University new business competition—a prize of forty-two thousand dollars. We were the first nonprofit, I think, ever to win it."

MEANS now has users in forty-nine states and counting. I asked Maria Rose to explain exactly how it works: "There is a casino in Rhode Island. They had about 350 pounds of I think it was clam chowder, grilled vegetables, and grilled chicken. They went to the MEANS website. And Todd, the chef at the casino, just typed in, 'I have 350 pounds of this. It fits these categories of food. I need somebody to come get it by the end of the week.' Our system automatically sent text messages and emails to all of the charities near the casino, and one of them claimed it. So eight minutes later, we had Amos House ready to go get it."

Brilliantly efficient. And at the core of her idea is a simple but powerful fact that she never forgets: "Hungry people can't think well. You can't strategize about getting a job, about finding a better one, about continuing your education, about taking care of your kids. You can't think about any of those things if you haven't eaten anything all day."

Her goal is taking care of all her fellow human beings. As Maria Rose says in her TED Talk, "Sometimes my job makes me feel like a walking anthology of sad stories." She shared the story of an elderly lady at a senior drop-in center who kept taking the ketchup packets from all the tables. Maria Rose noticed that the woman even fished unused packets from the trash.

"Why are you doing that?" Maria Rose finally asked the woman. She suspected she already knew why, but desperately hoped she was wrong.

"I use the packets and water them down to make ketchup soup on the days I don't have anything else to eat."

The woman was ninety years old.

DESPITE ALL THE amazing work she's done and the accolades she's earned, it was Maria Rose's next admission that really moved me.

"I think the first time I told somebody I wanted to kill myself, I was five. I've had pretty long-standing depression, and when medicated, things go pretty well, but I know very much what it means to feel like you do not have any worth or value, and the world is better off without you. And every time we do this, this is proof to depressed me that I'm not a net negative on the world."

Maria Rose is one of those remarkable forces of nature who has managed to deal with life and keep up her studies (as I mentioned earlier, she's studying to be a doctor as well as running her nonprofit) while also making the world a better place. Yet she's quick to credit others in helping to make MEANS a success.

"There's six of us full- and part-timers, and also volunteers. So there's a whole crew of us to do this insanity together. It's a lot of time management. I have a planner that is marked to the hour. I don't drink. I've never been to a frat party."

You have not missed anything, Maria Rose.

And just as Melissa listened to that fourteen-year-old

IONE BUTLER

with the big idea, Maria Rose revels in paying it forward. "One of my favorite parts of my job, other than the actual food going to people who need it, is giving the opportunity that I was given to younger students. So we will have high school–age volunteers and interns, and being able to give a fourteen-year-old girl the opportunity to work in a professional office environment all summer with a group of people who know what it is to be fourteen and smart enough to be functioning in a professional office? To be able to pass on that opportunity that I was given is the best thing in the world. I love that. And these kids soar. They're so smart. The interns and the volunteers that we get, we end up hiring a lot of them.

"The ones that hang on for a while, all they need is somebody who believes in them, who treats them like they matter and tells them it's okay for them to be who they are. When you're a really smart kid, or you're a gay kid, or you're an immigrant kid, or there's some way you don't fit in—you learn to hide that. So when you come into this environment, where suddenly they care deeply about you as a person, your gender identity and your sexual orientation is irrelevant. As soon as they know it's okay to be as smart as they are and be fully themselves, they just take off. It's awesome."

MEANS and Maria Rose Belding have helped countless hungry people—and made a few waves along the way, even being featured in a piece on *NBC Nightly News*. She knows the work she does is helping, but sadly, she can almost never share in the joy of seeing someone actually benefit from her labors. "We see the numbers, but we don't actually see the people we feed very often. And we got to see it in the NBC piece, and I bawled like a baby. You think that would get old, but it doesn't. I find so much hope in knowing that no matter how I may feel about myself at a given moment, there is value in what I have done."

What messages would she like you to take away from her story? Just remember that her wisdom is hard-earned. "We are not what has been done to us. Only what we have done for others. Whatever someone may have labeled you or called you, ultimately, you decide. Other people don't get to write your story."

TAKE ACTION

MARIA'S ADVICE IS, "Find your thing and do something. Because everybody sees so much injustice, and they want to fix it. We'd be a lot more efficient if people found the one thing that they feel the most bad about, that they are the most passionate about, and did something about that."

Following Maria Rose's lead:

1. Find the one thing you feel most passionate about, be it environmental protection, LGBTQ rights, child protection, human trafficking, helping the elderly, animal cruelty, etc.—

something that you want to see changed—
and write it down.

_____

_____

_____

_____

_____

_____

2. Make a list of five things you could do to
   make a difference for that cause. These actions could be researching a related charity,
   making a donation, signing up to be a volunteer, offering to help someone in need, etc.

   1. _____

   2. _____

   3. _____

   4. _____

   5. _____

3. Take action—do one of those five things right
   now.

4. Continue down the list until you've accomplished all five things, then see what more
   you can do.

KORIN SUTTON:
PLANT POWER

Florida native Korin Sutton had a pretty conventional up-bringing, so naturally, he ate meat—part of the stand-ard American diet, or SAD, as it is often called. What Korin and many Americans didn't know was that the famous food pyramid, introduced by the USDA in 1992 as a way to teach the proper way to structure your daily intake of food, was mostly a product of successful lobbying by organizations such as the American Meat Institute, the National Soft Drink Association, the Wheat Foods Council, and the Salt Insti-tute. (Yes, there used to be a salt institute. It was dissolved in 2019, in case you were wondering.)

After high school, Korin felt the call to serve his country, so he joined the US Marines. He loved being in the military. It gave him a strong feeling of purpose, and instilled in him tremendous discipline and confidence. But when he was de-ployed, it changed him in profound ways.

Korin quickly discovered that war was not like what you saw on TV and in movies—explosions and shooting and good guys versus bad guys. As an African American from the South who'd suffered racism and persecution, Korin realized that what he was seeing in Iraq was eerily familiar. In the Iraqis, he saw an entire people cast into poverty by war, their country a decimated landscape of chaos and suffering. He saw people who couldn't go to work even when they had a job, kids too afraid to venture outside their homes, let alone to school. He witnessed innocent fellow human beings thrust into a hellish nightmare by forces far beyond their control.

He began to see that the vision he'd had of such conflicts—as cut-and-dried, black-and-white, good versus evil—were not accurate. He thought about all the news coverage he'd watched of the gunfights and rocket attacks back in the States over the years, and realized people at home had no idea what war actually looked like. Suddenly, he began questioning everything—not just the righteousness of war, but the nature of reality, truth, and what we're told.

When he returned from Iraq, Korin joined the Navy Reserve and started college, majoring in criminal justice. Because of the wrongs he had seen while overseas in an active war zone, he wanted to do something about the injustice many people experience. As part of his studies, he took a persuasive speaking class, and one day, the class had a guest speaker who would change Korin's life forever.

His name was Gary Yourofsky, a well-known animal rights activist who became a vegan after taking offense to the practice of Detroit Red Wings fans throwing octopuses onto the ice during games. Gary called a local sports radio DJ and complained about the practice, saying it was wrong to use animals as props. The DJ, in an effort to point out Gary's hypocrisy, asked what Gary had eaten for dinner the night before. Gary lied, saying he'd eaten salad. But the moment he hung up the phone, he swore to himself it would be the shortest-term lie he ever told, and from that moment on, he has never eaten meat again.

Gary's work has gotten him arrested numerous times, but, he points out, Jesus, Rosa Parks, Gandhi, and Martin Luther King Jr. were also imprisoned for their beliefs. One of Gary's most famous stunts was breaking into a Canadian mink farm and releasing 1,542 of the tiny mammals, who were set to be slaughtered for their soft fur. He spent nearly three months in a maximum-security prison for that act of kindness.

While speaking to Korin's class, Gary laid out his case that harvesting living things, with eyes and limbs and feelings, is tantamount to a moral crime; he was especially fiery on the subject of factory farming.

Gary told the class that a corporation's sole aim is to make their products as desirable as possible to consumers. To that end, the meat industry spends billions of dollars each year on lobbyists, advertising, and public relations, while keeping the public in the dark about the animal torture involved and the effects of eating meat.

Korin hung on his every word.

Even beyond the rights of the animals themselves, Gary pointed out the startling burden of meat production on the world: significant air pollution from fossil fuel support of the meat industry, as well as a sizable portion of the world's methane pollution; wholesale deforestation to create more land for grazing; entire aquatic ecosystems becoming unbalanced or even disappearing due to overfishing—the list, sadly, goes on and on. Historically, humans have eaten meat since we lived in caves, but, Gary said, perhaps it's time to ask whether we really need to keep doing it, if the cost is so high.

Korin listened with his eyes wide and his jaw on the floor. He'd never thought twice about eating meat before, but Gary's points resonated with him. Having seen the mistreatment of prisoners in Iraq, Korin drew obvious parallels with the penned and caged animals Gary described, and it deeply disturbed him.

He walked out of the class and immediately switched his major from criminal justice to nutrition and physical sciences. Then he cracked the books and opened his mind, studying everything he could about the food system, diet, nutrition, and environmental health. He swore to follow a new path and do his part, not only for the sake of the earth and its creatures, but for his own health.

Korin began reading the works of Dr. Milton Mills and Dr. Michael Greger, two physicians who are powerful advocates of a plant-based diet and whose compelling supporting arguments are based on science.

Powerfully drawn to living a healthier lifestyle, Korin was determined to limit his dependence on animal protein, but wasn't quite ready to go full-on vegan. He became a pescatarian, looking to fish for protein, and began to experiment with recipes that embraced the vegan principles Gary had outlined. He changed his shopping habits, seeking healthier alternatives to what he'd been eating. He noticed a change in his physique right away, and kept track of his progress. His dogged experimentation began to pay off, as his healthy meals began to taste better. He also began serious weight training, another step toward total health commitment.

Gone was the old notion that vegetarians were pasty and puny, and that if you wanted to look like Arnold, you needed to wolf down porterhouse steaks like they were going out of style. In fact, Korin found the opposite to be true: he actually got stronger as his health regimen took him deeper and closer to a wholly plant-based diet. He also felt a sense of relief knowing that he was not contributing to the misery of fellow sentient beings.

Using his studies and intellect to guide him, he established his own parameters for nutrition, and began offering his services as a personal trainer. His only rule for clients was that they could not eat red meat, shellfish, or dairy. He switched to alternatives like almond milk and rice milk, which are also free of estrogen, given to cows to increase their milk production and found in most standard dairy milk as a result.

After a year as a pescatarian, he went full vegan, and saw an even more remarkable change when he looked in the mirror. In just three years, between 2009 and 2012, Korin, at five feet ten, went from 205 pounds to a very lean and mean 173 pounds . . . and actually got stronger! He had started his journey to new health as a fit man with around 17 percent body fat, but after a year on a plant-based diet, he was down to an astonishing 4 percent! He was completely jacked— competition-level shredded—and had never felt healthier. On top of that, his stamina and libido had improved, and his testosterone levels had increased.

Korin took part in some bodybuilding competitions, first as a hobby, then at a professional level, but now prefers to just stay super fit and maintain his online personal training business, which has a number of success stories from very happy (and healthier) clients. He keeps his clients on the straight and narrow by monitoring not only their workouts, but exactly what they eat, "because eighty percent of losing weight, or any type of fitness goal, really hinges on the food," he says. While he focuses on his clients' goals, primarily fat loss, his clients report other great side effects of their change in diet, including improved physical health, more energy, and feeling better overall.

PLANT-BASED DIETS are rapidly gaining social acceptance as more and more people are asking the same questions Korin did a decade ago. The move to meat alternatives can not only be better for your health—it's becoming big business. Korin admits that when he started eliminating meat, his options for meat substitutes were limited to little packs of "cold cuts" made by Tofurky, which were sometimes hard to find and always quite expensive. But that's all changing as retailers, both new and old, are discovering this exploding market. Major fast-food chains are introducing delicious plant-based offerings from Impossible Foods and Beyond Meat; Bill Gates has invested in the former, and the stock of the latter is doing well after a rocky start. (The best part? They taste great—I'm obsessed with the Impossible burger.) Go into the grocery store, and you'll find that the number of meat substitutes has jumped ten- or twentyfold in just the last year or two. Everywhere you look, there are new alternatives to meat, and with demand, prices will come down and quality will continue to improve.

KORIN WAS BY NO MEANS the first to jump on this bandwagon, but he represents a new generation of personal trainers and game-changers who are questioning what they've been told and why they've been told it. He has seized control of his own health and destiny, and is teaching others how to do it, too, spreading the word through his training and speaking at events. After serving his country with honor, he is now serving others and our planet by helping to improve the lives of his clients and all living things.

TAKE ACTION

1. Get educated: Check out the speech by Gary Yourofsky that caused Korin's turning point. Search for "Gary Yourofsky, best speech ever" to find it, or learn more at Gary's website, adaptt.org. Check out stud-

ies by Korin's other academic influences, Dr. Milton Mills and Dr. Michael Greger, and visit Dr. Greger's website, nutritionfacts.org. Read other research on nutrition and health, looking to credible researchers and organizations that are not being paid by special interests for their results. For example, many studies reporting that certain foods or beverages are good for you are often paid for by the industry that benefits from you being told that information.

2. If you're looking to get in shape or improve your health and are curious about switching to a plant-based diet, check out Korin's website, bodyhdfitness.com, where you'll find client testimonials, get real food hacks and recipes, and have access to meal plans, nutrition plans, and workout programs. And if you're interested in meeting and working with Korin directly, his offer is simple: "Set up an appointment. I'm willing to help you out."

3. Before you make any significant changes to your diet regimen, talk to your health provider.

PART 5

PURSUING YOUR PASSIONS AND PURPOSE

The most powerful weapon on earth is the human soul on fire.
—General Ferdinand Foch

H ave you ever asked yourself, *What am I doing with my life?* or *What's the point to all this?* Most people do at some point. But if it's a recurring theme for you, chances are, you're not doing the things you feel passionately about, or living your true purpose.

We all have unique gifts, talents, and skills, but they are often buried, lost, or forgotten. Growing up, we're told to pursue "sensible" careers rather than the creative or unconventional ones that might better serve our spirit. We learn to doubt our abilities, or get so caught up in paying the bills that we don't have the time or energy to do the things we really love. People throw around the acronym

YOLO ("you only live once"), but there's a lot to be said about the immeasurable value of that one life we're given.

In this chapter, you will meet people who ignored convention and pursued their passions. You'll learn about Kristin Finley, who abandoned her steady, lucrative engineering job to literally join the circus as a trapeze artist. There's Kenan Heppe, a chemist turned actor who packed up his life in LA to try his luck in China. And we'll kick it off with my own story, to show you how I got to where I am today, doing my best to walk the talk.

I hope these stories get you thinking about what truly excites you in life, and to start seeking out more of it.

Before we begin, take a moment to reflect on this question: What sets *your* soul on fire?

MY STORY:
CREATING A LIFE
BY DESIGN

B ack in November 2011, I was working as a receptionist, living paycheck to paycheck, like so many others. The workday was nine hours, and I had to commute an hour each way. My reward for all those hours was just £250 per week after taxes. (For perspective, that's less than four hundred US dollars. For more perspective, London is incredibly expensive, one of the priciest cities to live in in the world.)

I had been out of drama school for three years, and while I had a few acting jobs under my belt, my career wasn't advancing as much as I'd hoped. Every day consisted of waking up and going to work while it was still dark, then coming home when it was dark again. It was a depressing existence.

On one particular day, another in a seemingly endless series of gray, rainy winter days in London, I was sitting at my desk, trading Facebook messages with Tom Reed, an actor friend. Tom had booked a lead role on a prime-time CBS series, a mid-season replacement for *CSI: Miami* called *NYC 22*. Some of our mutual friends had gone out to visit him on set in New York City. I asked how he was getting on, and he told me he was having a blast—and that if it hadn't been such a pain getting a visa, he would have moved to the United States a lot sooner, as there were so many more roles and opportunities for actors of color there.

Tom's news ignited a fire in me. I'm eternally grateful to him for the motivation, because that was the moment I decided to move to LA. I knew I wouldn't be able to bear the New York winters after so much London gloom, and LA was the epicenter of the entertainment industry anyway. It also had palm trees and sunshine. It was going to happen.

I just wasn't sure how.

MY FATHER WAS BORN in the Bahamas, but has long been an American citizen. At first I thought it'd be easy for me to obtain a green card through him—and apparently, had I been under twenty-one, it would have been. However, because I wasn't, I would have to wait.

No problem, I thought.

Then I did a little more research. It turns out the US only issues a set number of green cards per year for the children of citizens over age twenty-one. To my astonishment, I found that people getting their green cards *right then* had been on that list for . . . wait for it . . . *eight years!* There was no way on earth I was going to live the status quo for the next eight years. My mind was made up; I was moving to LA. Now I just had to find another way to get to get there, one that wouldn't take almost a decade.

In February 2012, I set off on a monthlong trip to Los Angeles with a friend to see how I liked it. If I did, I would figure out how to obtain a visa that would allow me to live and work there. It was my first time being in LA as an adult, and I fell in love with it instantly. The weather, the lifestyle, the amazing contrasts in terrain—the mountains, the ocean, beaches, forests, deserts, even the vast, bustling city itself and the positive attitude of the people were so very welcome. As much as I love my hometown of London, Los Angeles, with its year-round sunshine and blue skies, was far better for my mental health.

During that trip, I connected with friends of friends, and met with an immigration lawyer to discuss my options. I also took some acting classes and managed to secure a manager who was willing to sponsor me for an O-1 visa, which would allow me to live and work as an actor in America. According to the US government, the O-1 visa is reserved for individuals who possess abilities in the sciences, arts, education, business, or athletics, or someone who has been recognized nationally or internationally in film or television.

I flew home smiling. My plan was coming together. I would spend the next few months gathering the required documentation and submitting my visa application to the US

Citizenship and Immigration Services. Six months later, the application was approved, and I readied myself to move.

It also worked out wonderfully that a friend of a friend who lived in the Hollywood Hills was going on a trip to Europe for five weeks and needed someone to watch her house and feed her cat while she was gone. So on September 16, 2012, with my life savings that amounted to $5,000 (and a few thousand more I'd gotten from selling my car and belongings and had set aside to buy a car), I was on my way to LA.

WHILE I WAS DELIRIOUS with excitement about all the new opportunities, my first few months in LA were an adjustment. I missed my friends and family, and had to start all over, building new relationships and finding work.

It took a while, but in early 2013 I got my first real break when I was cast as the character Susanna Moyer in *Ingress*, the augmented reality game that I mentioned earlier in Adam and Amanda's story. What was originally supposed to be a ten-week job lasted three and a half years and took me all over the world, attending in-person player events and filming *The Ingress Report*.

I was doing something that had never seemed possible in London: living off my acting. But as much as I loved the feeling of success and self-sufficiency, deep down I really wanted to be working on something that had more meaning and purpose. I also yearned to create something new rather than waiting to be cast in a role.

• • •

DEPRESSION IS SOMETHING I've experienced on and off throughout my life, so in 2015 I started a podcast, *Let's talk about* . . . (which later became *The Uplifting Content Podcast*) and began making videos about working through my challenges. Around that time, my godbrother in New Zealand tagged me in a Facebook post by Prince Ea, an influencer and content creator. Prince Ea was looking for actors in LA to be in his next video, a spoken-word piece about letting go of the labels we attach to ourselves and each other. My godbrother suggested I apply, and though I had no idea who this Prince Ea guy was, I remember thinking, *Why not? Let's see what it leads to.*

I sent a video audition, booked the job . . . and had one of the most eye-opening experiences of my life. I was blown away by Prince Ea's brilliance, beautiful videos, and powerful messages. He preached the importance of doing the things you were born to do and sharing your gifts with the world now, to avoid regret later in life.

We met on set and stayed in touch, and he encouraged me to keep making video content and my podcast. He shared the video I'd made about my experiences with depression with his many followers. It went viral, and I was not only inundated with messages from strangers thanking me for my honesty, but by friends suddenly confiding that they had often felt the same, and that I'd given them permission to drop their guard and share their feelings.

There is such shame around depression and mental illness, and it breaks my heart to think of the huge number who suffer alone when so many of us are going through the same thing. The positive feedback to my video gave me the courage to do more, and in March 2016, with Prince Ea's help, we launched an early version of *Uplifting Content* called *Unified Soul Theory*. A year later, it evolved into *Uplifting Content*, a platform designed to create and share content with the goal of inspiring people and providing a resource to anyone feeling depressed or low.

In the few years I've been running *Uplifting Content*, I've connected with incredible people and influencers and shared the work of creative forces like Jay Shetty, Goalcast, and Jason Silva. I've produced over 125 episodes of *The Uplifting Content Podcast* and interviewed guests including Gabby Bernstein, Mastin Kipp, Dr. Bruce Lipton, Greg Braden, journalist Johann Hari, former FBI hostage negotiator Chris Voss, and many other remarkable folks.

In 2017 I went on a three-month adventure around South America, taking suggestions from the *Uplifting Content* audience about where I should go and what I should do, and meeting up with some of them along the way.

This book came about after I reached out to some authors I knew to ask for their recommendations on literary representation. Aside from his career in the FBI, Chris Voss also authored a bestselling business book, *Never Split the Difference*. He loved my idea for this book, and connected me with his literary agent, whom I was honored and excited to sign with. It took about a year to get a book proposal together and to get it out to the world, and I was overjoyed when, in May 2019, it was picked up by Tiller Press, a new imprint of Simon & Schuster that was a perfect fit for *Uplifting Stories*.

This book, which I hope becomes an ongoing series, may have taken a while to come to fruition, but it has been well worth it for the stories I've been able to share with you about the remarkable people I've interviewed.

I KNEW FROM A YOUNG AGE that I didn't like being told what to do, so it would probably be best if, one day, I worked for myself. But I also knew that while it can be freeing to make your own decisions, it can also be scary. I wanted to have a positive impact on people, and I wanted the freedom and flexibility to travel the world on my own schedule. To do both, I needed to find ways of making money that didn't require reporting to an office every day.

A good friend once told me to "work smart, not hard," which has stuck with me. In this spirit, I constantly ask questions of people who are already doing what I want to do in an effort to learn how they got where they are. I'm naturally curious, so I've tried a lot of things, and I'll admit I've failed at many of them. But I always learn something, and I never give up on following my bliss. I "reverse-engineered" my life. By deciding how I wanted to live life first, I was able to make decisions and find work that would facilitate that. Here's how you can do the same if this approach appeals to you.

TAKE ACTION

WHAT KIND OF LIFE or career do you dream of? Do you want to be a homemaker, start a nonprofit, paint all day, or study marine animals in Hawaii? Here are the four simple steps I've used to achieve the things I wanted in life:

1. First and foremost, decide what you want. I think of goals like destinations in a GPS. You put in the address and set off on your journey; often you don't know where every twist and turn is taking you, but eventually you get there. Deciding what you want is like putting that end point into your mental GPS. When I decided to move to LA, or to start *Uplifting Content*, or to create this book, I knew without a doubt that these things would happen eventually. I entered the destinations in my mental GPS and set out on my journey to reach them.

2. Next, write it down. Consider this the first physical step toward your goal. Writing it out helps you break your goals down into manageable steps, set deadlines for each step, and see what you need to do next.

_____

_____

_____

_____

_____

_____

_____

3. Find the ways. Now you're in the discovery stage. Once you've decided what you want and have written it down, it's time to make it happen. There are infinite paths to achieving our goals, and to uncover yours, think outside the box, ask questions, and do your research. For example, I decided on that miserable day in the office in London that LA was going to happen. I then took a short trip to LA to confirm that I could thrive there. I met lots of new people and grilled them about everything—the cost of living, the vibe, the industry. Then I met with an immigration lawyer who told me what I needed to do to get the visa necessary to make it all happen. Once you know what is required and you've laid out all the essential steps in order, it's much easier to get there!

Also, get creative! During my trip to South America in 2017, I met Marc, who had gone to a port in Spain with a friend and asked if anyone needed help sailing across the Atlantic. He quickly found a taker and got a free ride across the ocean. (Apparently, this is a thing; search "boat hitchhiking" to learn more about it.) Along the way he met a German couple who asked him to join them in sailing from the Galápagos Islands to Australia—and this time, he was paid to help.

On that same trip, I met an Argentinean man who had converted a bus into a mobile hostel and was driving it all the way from Argentina to Alaska. He funded the trip by having guests stay in his hostel. I often hear people make excuses for why they can't do things, number one being "I don't have the money"—but you don't necessarily need a lot of money to do most things, if you are creative and frugal and work as you go.

4. Finally, to borrow from Nike, just do it. Let nothing stop you, delay you, or get in your way. Make the phone call, send the email, do the research. Fortune favors the bold!

KENAN HEPPE:
THE CHINESE CONNECTION

What do Bruce Lee and Kenan Heppe have in common? Everyone's heard of Bruce Lee, the martial artist and actor who, like James Dean, starred in only a handful of films, yet became a legend and an icon for successive generations of fans, actors, and martial artists. What most people don't realize is that he was actually born in the United States—in San Francisco, to be exact. His father, an opera singer, was on a yearlong US tour with a Chinese opera company, and soon after Bruce's birth, the family went home to Hong Kong.

As a child in Hong Kong, Bruce studied kung fu and started acting. He returned to the States at age eighteen, attended the University of Washington to study philosophy, got married and established several martial arts schools before ending up in Hollywood. He had some acting success, but for years mostly worked in the trenches, teaching his own martial arts creation, which he called Jeet Kune Do. His big break didn't come until he moved to back to Hong Kong in 1971.

And the rest is history.

Now, back to Kenan Heppe. You may not have heard of him yet, but like Bruce Lee, Kenan is an American actor who knocked around in Hollywood for a few years and while he's had the occasional success he hadn't had his big break. Unlike Bruce, Kenan is not Asian, but rather a Caucasian chap from Oregon. He is also no martial artist, though he is a fantastic piano player. But Kenan, like Bruce, saw his life change for the better when a series of events led to his pulling up stakes in Los Angeles and moving to China to act in films. And we're not talking just a gig here and there— Kenan became one of just a few Western actors to head East and become known in the Chinese entertainment business.

American, Kenan Heppe is a rising Chinese star.

How do I know about this mysterious Westerner who has so captivated one of the world's largest film markets?

Kenan is a very good friend of mine, and his story is for anyone interested in stepping into the unknown to pursue their passion. He's spent many years and traveled thousands of miles in search of his.

FIRST, KENAN HEPPE is a really smart guy. You figure that out about thirty seconds after meeting him. Like most actors,

Kenan was expressive and creative as a kid, but he was also very practical—he got that from his parents. He always knew he would go to college, regardless of what he ended up doing as a career. His father, a scientist, was willing to cover the cost of a good education, citing college as being "the best predictor for career success."

Kenan excelled in chemistry, so that became his major. His other passion was acting, and since acting is not always a parent's favorite career choice, Kenan, being the genius that he is, came up with a rather unique proposition. His father was keen for him to attend an Ivy League school, but Kenan suggested that instead of his parents spending $50,000 a year on tuition at an Ivy, he could enroll at a state university and save them a ton of money. He further suggested that if he graduated at the top of his class with a 4.0 GPA, he should be allowed to use the money he'd saved them for a deposit to buy an apartment in Los Angeles so he could pursue acting work. He promised his father that if acting didn't work out, he would sell the apartment and give his parents back their money—plus, he'd have a career in chemistry to fall back on. It was a win-win. He and his dad shook on it, and Kenan enrolled at Oregon State University.

EVEN FOR SOMEONE as smart as Kenan, college wasn't a walk in the park. Not long after he started classes at Oregon State he was diagnosed with Lyme disease, and spent his freshman year in bed attached to an IV. But with his drive and ambition, he didn't let that incredible inconvenience get in his way.

Four years later, Kenan walked out with a chemistry degree and the honor of being the first Oregon State chemistry undergrad in fifteen years to graduate with a perfect 4.0 GPA. Three days later, he packed up his things and was on the road to Tinseltown.

With no connections in Los Angeles, he started making money as a math and chemistry tutor, and studied acting in his spare time, taking as many acting classes as he could. (In fact, that's how we met: in an acting class in 2015.)

One afternoon, while scrolling through his social media feed, Kenan saw a picture of two kittens who needed adopting. "Without thinking," he says wryly, "I said I'd give them a home." Unbeknownst to him at the time, this was the first in a series of events that would lead to his big break.

Ina, an Austrian actress, showed up with the kittens and casually mentioned that she did acting work in China. It piqued Kenan's interest, because he'd taken an introductory Mandarin course in college. He'd always been curious about China and felt drawn to learning more about it, but never pursued it further because chemistry had begun to consume his time in college, and then he moved to California. He demonstrated a little Mandarin for Ina; she was impressed, and told him there were acting opportunities for Westerners willing to move to China and brush up on the language. (For the uninitiated, China's film and television industry is huge, and garners around $100 billion in revenue per year.)

Ina gave Kenan the phone number for a middleman in China who helped foreigners get acting work there. It was an intriguing idea, but he put the phone number in a drawer and forgot about it.

A few years later, Kenan was still struggling to make it in Hollywood, and he came to a stark realization: as a white guy in America, he was not in demand. With the recent push for greater diversity in TV and film (a cause he fully supported), he had been told on more than one occasion he was "too white. A mid-twenties white guy. Dime a dozen. You're untouchable now." It stung, but he persevered.

He did find some success in LA, getting a role on a soap opera and in a Lay's potato chip commercial. And around this time, about a year after we met in that acting class, Kenan asked me to be part of a web series he had created called *Girlfriend Guy*. In the series, Kenan plays a hopeless romantic who is also quite a pushover, and I play his mean girlfriend. It's a very dysfunctional relationship with a healthy dose of conflict, and we had a great time making it. People love it; many viewers think we're a real couple. (You can find the videos on our Facebook page, www.facebook.com /girlfriendguy.)

Girlfriend Guy was becoming very popular, and an old high school crush from his hometown who had seen it reached out saying she wanted to reconnect, and asked if she could come visit Kenan in LA. He was over the moon. "I thought, 'It's happening! I'm doing what I love, making things people like, I feel fulfilled, and women are feeling more attracted to me! Wow!' So I planned a romantic weekend: comedy shows, suave Italian restaurants, a little boat ride, etc. Of course none of it ever happened, because she canceled the night before," he says. It turned out his old flame had met someone else in Oregon. Kenan was deflated.

With his weekend suddenly opened up, he booked a session with his acting coach. And it just so happened that as he was going to meet his coach—the exact time he would have been going to pick up his date from the airport, had she not canceled—he bumped into a friend, Kenny Leu, in the parking lot. Fate's second intervention.

Kenny mentioned that he was helping a local casting agency. They were auditioning actors who could speak Mandarin for an upcoming Chinese production, and Kenny was serving as a reader for the actors being considered. Kenan recalled some of his Mandarin from the short course he'd taken years before, and asked Kenny, *"Ni hui shuo zhongwen ma?"* (You speak Chinese?) Kenny's eyes bulged in astonishment. "What the *bleep*, Kenan! You speak Mandarin?"

Kenan explained that he'd taken a little Mandarin in college, with emphasis on "a little." Kenny wouldn't have it, and told Kenan his tones were amazing. (Mandarin is a tonal language, one in which the pitch with which a syllable is spoken changes its meaning, making it very difficult to learn and speak.) "He guaranteed me that if I could memorize lines, I could get this role," Kenan said. "The casting office had been searching three months for a young white male actor who could speak Mandarin. They searched all of New York, but couldn't find one. All of LA, but couldn't find one." All he had to do was learn the lines and send in a taped audition.

Kenan soon learned that there were maybe four or five professionally trained Western actors in his look and age category who could speak enough Mandarin to make their way through a production. He went from being just another white guy in a sea of white guys just like him to being a pearl of great price. He was suddenly in demand . . . in China.

He knew he could learn the lines. Memorizing complex strings of equations got him through chemistry in college. He'd had enough of a taste of Mandarin to know he could do the same.

In no time, he sent his tape off to the casting director, and the next day, just as his friend Kenny had assured him, he was offered the job. They booked him a ticket to fly to New York to film a supporting role in the Chinese movie *Love Is a Broadway Hit*. Kenan is now grateful to his old crush for backing out of their weekend, because if she hadn't, he'd not have bumped in to Kenny and been cast in that role leading to the many others that followed.

When the movie was set to debut in China, Kenan thought it would be a good idea to go there early, plant himself, and try to find other opportunities. But two things stood in his way: he needed someone to take care of his cats, and he didn't know anyone in China. Then he remembered the phone number Ina had given him for that middleman, and took it out of the drawer he'd left it in. He made arrangements to send his cats home to Oregon and packed his bags for China.

At the airport in China, he swapped out his US SIM card and punched in the middleman's number, praying someone would answer. They did, and in his best Mandarin, he said, "Hi, I'm Kenan and I'm American. I'm an actor. I don't know what I'm doing. Can you help?"

Two weeks later, he was shooting a TV show in the Chinese jungle. Kenan told me, "In a moment of caring for others—in this case, thinking purely about the cats needing a home, and not about how difficult it would sometimes be to raise them—I received the most important phone number of my young adult life."

CHINESE PRODUCTIONS, as it turns out, are very different to Hollywood productions. Kenan had to adjust to this new way of doing things, and quickly. Since he was not yet fluent in Mandarin, the production hired a Chinese/English interpreter. Unfortunately, Kenan discovered that in an effort to save money, they'd hired an interpreter who actually spoke no English!

There were some other growing pains early on. Kenan was not at all familiar with the Chinese film industry and literally didn't know who anyone was. One day he was to film a scene with a Chinese actor. Kenan suggested they work on the actor's English line—he thought it could be better. The crew was in shock and couldn't believe he'd spoken to his co-star that way. Kenan, it turned out, was speaking to Guo JingFei, one of the biggest stars in Chinese cinema, a Brad Pitt–level celebrity, and he had no idea! Fortunately they're now good friends, which Kenan believes is partly due to his genuine interaction with the man.

From then on, Kenan made it a point to research exactly who it was he'd be starring with.

He took his new career direction seriously, and laid out a plan for success. He decided that if his leaving LA was going to have meaning, he would have to put in the kind of hard work that had gotten him perfect grades in chemistry. He immersed himself in learning Mandarin, knowing that it would make him a more valuable commodity. It was not only his ticket in, but his ticket to stay. In the six months before his film was released, he spent eight hours a day, five days a week, with a Mandarin teacher. It took him over eight months to approach fluency.

Kenan's language classes paid off, and as his Mandarin improved, so did the parts offered to him. Now that he could operate on the set and in society, the moments of confusion and miscommunication were happening less often.

His dream was coming true, only in an entirely different way than he'd imagined it. He was supporting himself as an *actor*—not a tutor—challenging his mind and body by pursuing his profession in an ancient and beautiful culture. His heart, mind, and soul were all challenged and fulfilled. It was working out far better than he'd expected.

Then one day, it all fell apart.

His parents phoned. Their voices agonized, they managed to get out the details: they'd found his younger brother's body in the water.

It was suicide.

Kenan knew his brother had battled depression and anxiety—he had suffered from bipolar disorder—but he wrestled with what must have been going through his brother's mind as he took his life. On top of Kenan's own feelings of loss, he couldn't bear to think of the pain his parents were in, and immediately flew back to the US to be with his family. The months that followed were the worst he'd ever experienced. "Devastation found its way through every aspect of my life," he said.

About seven months after his brother's death came his father's birthday. Since his father had spent his life making his children's dreams come true, Kenan wanted to do something kind for him, to help relieve some of the trauma.

While his father had taken the family to exotic locations when they were kids, he'd never gotten to his own dream destination: the Grand Canyon. Kenan took his parents there, despite his own revulsion for sun, canyons, and heights, all of which are in abundance at Arizona's mile-deep gorge. Wanting to share the geological marvel, Kenan made a short video for his 700,000 followers on social media back in China.

One of those followers happened to be a film director's wife who wanted to make a film about Edgar Snow, a Missouri-born journalist who, fascinated with China, journeyed there in the late 1920s and wrote about the turmoil of the time. The Chinese revere Snow because he was the first Western journalist to meet and interview Mao Zedong, who would become the country's leader. Snow spent several months with Mao, and his resulting book, *Red Star Over China*, is a de facto biography of Mao, as well as an analytical impression of what the Chinese were trying to accomplish by embracing and evangelizing Communism.

So far, the producers had had no luck finding the right actor to play Edgar Snow—until the director's wife saw Kenan's Grand Canyon video and thought Kenan was a dead ringer for Snow.

Again, opportunity had rewarded him while he was looking out for others—first the kittens, then his dad.

The director arranged to fly Kenan to Sichuan. They told him he was the guy—his look was perfect, his Chinese was good—but he'd have to wait while the film found investors. It was agony.

Temptation and fate were also conspiring against Kenan as he waited for the film's financing to come through. He was offered $50,000 to play the lead in a Chinese web series for three months. So now his choice was to take the sure thing and risk losing the movie, or turn down the money and . . . wait?

Fifty grand is a sizable amount, and it forced Kenan to think hard about why he was in this business. Was it about money? *Just* money?

No.

That was his final answer. "I was in this for the pursuit of meaning, and for art, and for joy."

He turned down the web series, and resolved to wait for the movie to be financed. He waited a month. Then two months. Two became three. His money running low; some days he ate only peanut butter and drank water. Finally, after four long months, the production called. They had the money.

Three months later, he was standing alone in Tiananmen Square.

He was filming the final scene in *The Secret of China*, a story important to his adopted countrymen. Kenan Heppe, an American from Oregon, was also entering a very, very exclusive club: Westerners who've played the lead in a Chinese feature film.

KENAN IS NOW in two traveling stage productions, *That Physics Show* and *That Chemistry Show*, where he uses his scientific knowledge to perform experiments onstage in Broadway-style splendor—all in Chinese, of course. He has over a million followers on Chinese social media, and, he says, "Once in a while I get very decent roles in TV shows or films."

He's fully engaged in doing what he loves, but it took hard work and some lucky breaks to get there. The cultural hurdles and language barrier made it more difficult, yet at the same time, those were the reasons many other American actors have not tried for roles in Chinese films, giving him an opening. He still doesn't have an agent, so he has to negotiate for himself, and as a foreigner, he gets treated differently. But if the deal he proposed to his dad back before college is any indication, he probably doesn't need help negotiating.

I couldn't be more proud of him for taking a leap of faith, working hard to learn a new language, and finding success in a foreign land.

The message he wants to leave you with is, to not chase happiness, but instead try to find meaning and joy in the things around you and in what you are doing because happiness—and life—can be fleeting.

TAKE ACTION

KENAN'S SUGGESTED actions are twofold. Here they are, in his words:

FIRST: The meeting.

If you're not doing what you love, gather the people closest to you, family, friends, and loved ones, and explain clearly and honestly what you wish you were doing. Sometimes those closest to you do not know your innermost dreams, especially if you've never expressed them or have done so in a way they may not realize was serious. Say, "Did you know this about me? Did you know that this is what I would actually love to be doing?"

My family knew that I wanted to be an actor since I was a kid, so it was not news.

See what the reaction is and who is supportive and who is not. Also, expect suggestions and comments, and give your audience an opportunity to express themselves. What they say could be a big help in shaping your direction and finding your true path. Who knows? They might even help push you in a direction you didn't consider but that gets you to your goal.

SECOND: Be realistic.

I would love to be a professional basketball player. NBA. Yeah. However, I have some shortcomings. The first is that I'm literally too short, notwithstanding the even shorter five-foot-seven Spud Webb, who had an insane shot. I do not have an insane shot. In fact, my shot is far too sane. I have no three-point shot, no two-point . . . no one-point. I'm also not built for it. No ball-handling skills. Nope. Nada. It would never work.

It's nice to say it and wish for it, but it's just not true that everyone can do anything they put their mind to. I'm not going to give birth for example. Wrong gender, wrong plumbing. Point is, find something that there is *an actual possibility of you doing*. I'm not saying you have to pick something easy.

Pick the possible.

KRISTIN FINLEY:
LIVING WITHOUT A NET

You're climbing a very skinny ladder that seems to go forever. When you get to the top, there's not much there to reassure you—just a small platform, about the size of a step, and some ropes you can use to steady yourself as you climb onto it. You're more than twenty feet above the ground. You've never really had any fear of heights, but you do have a healthy respect for gravity, and you know that twenty feet is plenty high enough to leave a mark. The platform is a little wobbly.

There's a net spread out beneath you, but it doesn't inspire much confidence. It doesn't look as big as it did from the ground, but at least it means that if you fall, you'll gently bounce a few times rather than going splat. That's good, you muse. You look over at the object of your focus, a trapeze, held on the other side by a friendly looking person.

He releases the trapeze so you can grab for it. It hits your hands, you wrap them around it . . . and you're airborne. In the few seconds it takes to reach the far platform, you realize something. This isn't scary. It's fun. Insanely fun.

You're hooked.

This is what happened to Kristin Finley the first time she tried the trapeze. She had a great, secure, lucrative engineering job at the time—and was unaware that she would eventually make the extraordinary decision to quit that job and join the circus.

KRISTIN WAS BORN in Los Angeles, and was raised by a very strict but loving father. After high school, she went right into the military. She credits her service for giving her a great sense of order and discipline, and believes everyone could benefit from at least two years in a similar environment.

The military gave her a chance to travel and learn a technical trade. She ended up stationed in New Mexico as a mechanic on the then top-secret F-117 Nighthawk stealth fighter. "That was amazing," she recalls. "It was super cool, and I learned a lot." But the work kept her mostly in the US, and she yearned to explore the world.

She left the military and got a job repairing helicopters at Van Nuys Airport, then as a mechanic at the Anheuser-Busch facility. While working for Anheuser-Busch, Kristin was back in her hometown living with her father, but traveling to all the other breweries to train technicians how to fix and maintain their new gear helped scratch her travel itch for a while. Then, four years into the job, she got shattering news. Her father was very sick, diagnosed with an aggressive form of cancer. In the final stages of his fight, Kristin's dad made it clear that he wanted to be in the house he shared with his daughter and not a hospital. He died at fifty, less than two years after his initial diagnosis.

After he passed, Kristin "didn't want to be in the house. There's just so much hurt and pain." So she sought out hobbies and after-work activities to keep her mind off things and her body out and about. She started archery classes, then got her rotary wing license so she could fly the helicopters she already knew how to fix. One day a coworker and friend mentioned something Kristin had never even considered before.

"I'm sorry, but you said you're taking trapeze classes?" Kristin asked.

Her friend nodded.

Kristin was intrigued, and asked if she could come to a class and watch. She went with the friend to a trapeze class in Woodland Hills, a suburb of Los Angeles, where she immediately recognized the famous "Candy Cane Lane," a street where all the neighbors deck out their houses for the holidays with lights and decorations. One house in particular had always caught her eye: its front yard featured Santa on a trapeze, catching Mrs. Claus as she flies into his arms. Naturally, this was the house where the trapeze classes were held. Kristin was charmed to discover a huge trapeze rig in the backyard.

To her delight, the instructors asked if she wanted to do more than just watch, and from her first swing, Kristin knew she'd found something special. Soon she was a regular member of the class. She abandoned her other activities to pay for it, and it became her whole life outside of work. Then one day, about two years in, her status as an amateur changed.

Some acquaintances from class had a show called the Sky Circus, and they invited Kristin, along with her trainer and his girlfriend, to attend. After the performance, they asked if they'd like to perform at the next day's show.

"We thought they were joking," admits Kristin. But they weren't. That was Kristin's first gig as a paid trapeze artist, and she knew it was something she wanted to pursue professionally.

But was it was even possible? she wondered. She was a pretty pragmatic person, and it was difficult to make the mental leap required. So for a while, she pondered it, working the graveyard shift at the brewery and taking trapeze classes during the day.

Then fate intervened. She got an offer to go on the road for three months with the world-famous Ringling Bros. Circus, filling in for another performer. Kristin didn't hesitate; she took a three-month leave of absence from Anheuser-Busch and packed her bags.

Her seemingly crazy dream was now her new reality.

• • •

WHEN SHE GOT BACK after three months, she knew she was at a crossroads. She loved her job as a brewery mechanic and deeply appreciated the steady paycheck, but the lure of a life on the road was too strong. Trapeze had become, more than anything else, her life's joy.

This desire to do something as exciting and exotic as trapeze for a living coincided with another revelation that hit close to home and helped in her decision. Her dad had always been sort of a homebody. When he had time off from work, he would either stay home or head to Northern California to fish with a friend. He'd only been on one cruise in his life.

But Kristin had other dreams and a burning need to travel, so she decided she would do just that. This was Kristin's big inflection point, the chance to go on the road again, this time not servicing breweries but rather flexing her new skills as a circus trapeze artist. While she didn't have a gig lined up after the Ringling job, she knew it was now or never.

"I'm going to smell the roses," she decided, and handed in her notice at work.

I asked how it felt to make the big decision. "It was terrifying, terrifying," she says. "Because I was going from the secure job making great benefits, paid vacation, security, and I could live in my house and I had a Lexus." She knew most people would think she was crazy to walk away from such security, but as she told me, "You can't take anything with you. The only things you have are your memories and the relationships you build with people. That's what's important to me."

Now jobless, she began calculating how she could make her new career path work. Living in the entertainment capital of the world, she saw stunt performing as a natural way to supplement her income. She got her Screen Actors Guild (SAG) card and began booking stunt jobs, doing what she had to do to make a name for herself in that field, from having the requisite headshots taken to making a demo reel of her stunts. She dipped into her 401(k) to finance it all.

Meanwhile, as she waited for the circus to call, she finally found the strength to clear out her dad's possessions in the house, something she'd struggled for years to do. She gave a lot of them away to friends, including her father's treasured record collection. By then she'd pared her life down to bare bones; her debts were paid, and all she had left were some small utility bills and her cat. That's when the call came in for her first big job: a circus troupe was mounting a show in Florida and needed her. Despite the job not starting immediately, Kristin grabbed her cat, jumped in the car, and headed east to the Sunshine State.

Even though she was weeks early, she began practicing and found that Florida's high summer humidity had softened her hands so much that her first session on the trapeze left her hands chewed and bloody. Gritting her teeth, she bandaged them and continued working out her routines with her fellow artists, stepping up her workouts to twice a day.

Then, just before the tour, she got disturbing news: The

family at the core of the show had split up. The two brothers and their wives had had some sort of disagreement and gone their separate ways.

Disappointed, the now diminished troupe decided the show must go on, and they headed to their first location in Virginia to begin dress rehearsals. One of the highlights of the original show had been a triple somersault, but now, with the key artists absent, there was no one skilled enough to perform such an advanced stunt. Kristin was aware that the troupe had committed to that particular trick in their contract, but went ahead with their first show, which was a sort of preview for the rest of the tour. At this point, they'd been practicing most of the summer and had not been paid a dime.

After the show, Kristin's boss called her to his trailer. The news was bad: the troupe had been fired. A new artistic director decided to go in a different direction, and without the triple somersault, they had lost their draw for the promoters. While it was a shock to have her first gig go so sideways, she chalked it up to life in the circus. Less than two months later, she was offered a job in UK working for the Netherlands National Circus. Her career as a trapeze artist was in full swing, and she never looked back.

KRISTIN HAS ACCEPTED the way the industry operates, and works around it. All the performers are independent contractors. The jobs can be anything from circus tours to events like a baseball game, a fair, or even a concert. Event promoters pay a flat fee that gets divvied up by the performers. Depending on how many people are involved, it can get pretty lean.

She has to cover her own expenses on the road, gas and food and whatever else she needs. She admits it can be a hard life, but she's been happy doing it for nearly fifteen years. And she's now shifting her focus to another facet of circus art that has less competition and pays very well because it's a lot more dangerous: human cannonball.

Traditionally, circus acts were mostly created by and stayed within families. The reason was twofold: so you knew in whose hands you were putting your life, and so you could generally depend on your colleagues to hang around and keep the act going. Kristin understands that notion, but she also feels that family can be greater than blood relatives. Tired of splitting money with larger troupes of performers, she now travels with her own small troupe, consisting of her boyfriend, another couple, and, of course, her cat.

When I interviewed her, she was laid up in Tulsa, Oklahoma, nursing a broken leg. This setback was temporary, but it kept her out of work. She'd already turned down three contracts and was restless to get back in action . . . and keep the money flowing.

She says she has considered getting a "regular" job again, but is still enjoying what she's doing. While it's by no means glamorous, she would never give up all the places she's traveled to, the experiences she's had, and the people she's met. She often thinks of her dad, and living her bliss on the road is her tribute to him.

Kristin would be the first to tell you that quitting a steady job to pursue your dreams won't always be a walk in the park; in fact, it can get downright frightening. But it may also be the best thing for you. Kristin came up with a name for the chapter of her life after her dad passed away: her "Super Happy Fun Adventure Time." It's her reminder to live life to the fullest, because you never know how long you have.

Her message to you is simple: "Don't be afraid to try something new, whether you succeed or fail. Don't put limits on yourself. Find what you love and do it."

She certainly has, and you can, too.

TAKE ACTION

WE LIVE IN THE information age, so there's no excuse not to find ways to explore your passions. Learn about or get involved with something you think you'll enjoy. To find affordable classes in subjects like salsa, yoga, trapeze, arts and crafts, or cooking, look to sites like LivingSocial and Groupon. If you'd like to be part of group activities like a choir, a sports group, or a book club, or find a group to go hiking or camping or otherwise travel with, try Meetup.com or Facebook groups. And, of course, don't forget YouTube.com, where there are how-to videos on everything you can possibly imagine.

What is something you're passionate about or would like to get better at or do more of?

_____

_____

_____

_____

_____

_____

FIND A WAY TO MAKE IT HAPPEN!

PART 6

THE UNIMAGINABLE

Whether you believe you can do a thing or not
you are right.
—Henry Ford

You've probably heard a therapist or life coach use the phrase "limiting beliefs." These are the beliefs that hold us back, contain us, keep us playing small, and stop us from reaching our full potential. Unfortunately, many of us have them, and they can be toxic and destructive if we do not confront them.

The most common limiting belief? "I'm not good enough."

Another might be "All rich people are evil," which can stop you from making money and achieving financial freedom. Believing "Most new businesses fail" may hold you back from starting a business or a side hustle. "People can't be trusted" may leave you feeling lonely and lacking connections with others. The belief "You must work hard to survive" can leave you with little time to enjoy the fruits of your labor.

But why do we have limiting beliefs, and where do they

come from? I interviewed Dr. Bruce Lipton, a stem cell biologist and leader in a study of consciousness, for *The Uplifting Content Podcast*. He explained that we are all programmed with a set of beliefs from a very young age. As we get older, we find examples that validate those beliefs in our lived experiences, so by the time we're grown-up adults, the beliefs are so ingrained in our subconscious that we're often not even aware of them.

So how can we identify our limiting beliefs or "faulty programs?" Dr. Lipton explains that if what you want in life constantly shows up easily, it's a good sign that you have a positive program about it. For example, if you have a great set of friends whom you trust, it means you've got a good subconscious program about how you relate to others, fit in, and make friends. But if the things you want in life are not manifesting for you, or there are areas of life in which you have persistent problems, it is a strong indication that you have limiting beliefs around those things.

After speaking to Dr. Lipton, I set out on a mission to uncover my own limiting beliefs. And there were a few! One was that there is no man in the world right for me—and surprise, surprise, I was always single. Another was that no one wanted to hear what I had to say, which was holding me back from sharing content. There were many others, which I shall not bore you with.

I urge you to take a minute to think about and write down some of your limiting beliefs. It takes a good amount of self-awareness to do this, but by looking at what you want but haven't managed to make happen, or the areas where you consistently struggle (work? love? family?), you can begin to identify the faulty program getting in your way.

SO HOW DO YOU change your limiting beliefs?

1. The first step, as I outlined above, is to identify your limiting beliefs and write them down.

2. Recognize that these are your beliefs, not absolute truths. For me, the belief that there is no one right for me on earth is pretty ridiculous, and obviously untrue. Look at your beliefs and ask yourself, *Are these absolute truths?*

3. Go through your list of limiting beliefs and replace them with empowering new ones. For example, I could replace, "I can't write" (another limiting belief of mine!) with "I'm doing my best by putting pen to paper every day, working with people who can help, and getting better the more I do it."

4. A very simple way of changing your beliefs is by listening to a guided meditation or hypnosis about whatever it is you want to change—be it having more money, confidence, or better health or relationships. By listening to audio

about this right before you go to sleep or as you're waking up, your brain is in the theta wave (healing or cosmic) state, which is optimal for self-hypnosis. This is when you can really tap into your subconscious and replace your limiting beliefs with better ones.

I wanted to touch on the importance of the positive power of beliefs, because the stories you're about to hear might seem literally unbelievable. But in fact, they're wonderful examples of what people can achieve, so prepare for your jaw to drop and your mind to be blown.

In this chapter you'll learn about Daniel Kish, a blind man who can "see," and Troy James, who found stardom and fame with his ability to contort his body in the most seemingly inhuman and disturbing ways. And finally, you'll read about Kyle Maynard, a quadruple amputee who lets nothing hold him back and who has climbed two of the world's highest mountains, Mount Kilimanjaro and Mount Aconcagua . . . without the aid of prosthetics!

I hope the stories of these awe-inspiring people leave you charged up and ready to discover what's possible.

DANIEL KISH:
THE BLIND MAN
WHO SEES

A man on a bicycle speeds down a hill at full tilt, his face a mask of pure concentration. He pedals hard and steers with complete focus; you can tell he knows exactly where he's going. As he passes, you notice an odd clicking regularly punctuating the air, like one insect signaling another. You look around and see nothing but the man and his bike, receding into the distance. Suddenly, you realize that he's the source of that curious noise. The clicking sounds are how he "sees," because the man is blind.

In fact, *he has no eyes.*

BY THE TIME Daniel Kish was thirteen months old, he had lost both eyes to cancer. His parents were initially devastated by his diagnosis, an aggressive retinoblastoma. But when it became clear that he would survive, the loss of his vision seemed almost a small price to pay for his life. Feeling that their son may have already dodged his biggest bullet so young, his parents made a conscious choice to raise him differently than most other blind children: instead of hovering around him, protecting him, they would simply let him *be a kid*.

Though they were young parents and neither had a college education, they were free thinkers, as Daniel puts it. Their biggest fear was raising him to be incapable of living as an independent adult. Luckily, they would soon discover that fear was not in Daniel's character. After the doctors had removed his second eye, the impatient toddler escaped from his hospital crib and began wandering around the intensive care unit, "probably looking for whoever did that to me," Daniel wryly notes.

His lack of eyes didn't seem to slow him down. In fact, a powerful drive to keep moving, to never let anything hold him back, is one of Daniel's defining qualities.

DANIEL WAS BORN in 1966, a time when it was assumed that anyone who was blind would eventually be handed over to professional care. But his parents defied convention. They didn't instantly trust the "blindness professionals" who pressured them to surrender Daniel's freedom for a guarantee of his safety.

Back then, there was a great deal of institutional discrimination that made it difficult for someone with a blind person in the family to own or even rent a home, because no one wanted to insure them.

Fortunately, Daniel's parents understood that ignorance and fear were "matters of the mind, and the mind is adaptable," he says. They understood the power of expectations, that if you or someone else thought you couldn't do something, then you probably couldn't. They were also careful not to let him feel their own concerns. They were fully aware that blindness would pose a significant challenge for Daniel, but they had unshakable faith that he would triumph over his blindness, one day moving out, "paying taxes," and facing the world head on, just like everyone else.

They just weren't sure how.

Daniel's answer would be something they never could have imagined. He would find a way around his loss that would astound everyone.

WHEN DANIEL WAS about eighteen months old, his parents noticed he was making a strange clicking sound by pressing his tongue against the roof of his mouth and snapping it quickly, creating a tiny but sharp noise. Most people just assumed it was odd tic from an unconventional child. In truth, Daniel was beginning to develop his own new form of vision. He understood at a very young age that the barrier between him and his freedom was being able to "see" the world around him.

His solution was to borrow from bats.

The images our eyes show us are actually just light—electromagnetic radiation—reflecting off objects, defining them in shapes and colors, near and far. Sound can define objects in a manner similar to light. The technical word for what Daniel was doing is echolocation, the science of locating objects by reflected sound. While bats are the best known echolocators, a few birds, some whales, dolphins, and even rats and shrews use sound to "see."

But how does a human do it? And how did a child younger than two years old come upon it?

"I learned to click my tongue and communicate with my surroundings. That a child would just spontaneously learn to do that might seem improbable, but it actually isn't if you consider how children naturally adapt," Daniel says.

Daniel had invented his own way of seeing *without eyes*.

When his elementary school phoned to complain about Daniel's clicking, his mother said, "Too bad. He needs to know what's around him, and that's how he does it."

When Daniel was brought home by the police for climbing a neighbor's fence, his mother shrugged it off. Yes, he would occasionally bump into things, but he could walk to school, cross busy streets, and make his way in the world all on his own.

By six, he had upped the ante on his intrepid mother's fears: riding a bike! Using a retaining wall to guide him at first, he had to flood his environment with a barrage of clicks . . . but he found he could do it.

The child with no eyes was actually *riding a bike*!

Of course, there were mishaps. One day he crashed into a telephone pole, and "there was blood everywhere," he says. He knocked out his front teeth running into another pole at school. He jokes about one occasion, a few years later, when a rambunctious soccer shed leapt into his path and "just destroyed my mouth."

Another major influence on Daniel's behavior was perhaps even more damaging: the warfare at home. His father took his anger out on Daniel's mother. With her life ruled by constant fear, she vowed not to let her sons, especially her blind one, be guided by negative emotions. She looked for a way out of the relationship and the torment it caused her.

This constant combat shaped the way Daniel reacted to the world. He was more interested in physically expressing himself, climbing trees or running around to burn off the stress from home, rather than sitting quietly in school.

When his mother finally found the courage to leave her husband, Daniel was around eight, and a pretty tough kid. Daniel admits he enjoyed high-intensity physical exertion, even roughhousing, but he avoided popular team sports like baseball or soccer "because silent flying projectiles weren't really my thing back in those days."

Understandable.

THINGS CHANGED when Daniel met Adam, the first other blind person he'd ever known. Adam enrolled in Daniel's school in the fifth grade, after attending a school for the blind where he was used to having others do everything for him. Adam ran into walls and had trouble doing the simplest things.

At first, Daniel was baffled by this. He would complain to his mother that Adam seemed unable to do anything, and it vexed him. Adam represented everything Daniel, as a blind person, had sought to reject, and when others began to lump them together as "the blind kids," it enraged him. He began bullying Adam, making fun of him around the other kids, directing cruel jokes at him, and even beating him up on a few occasions.

Time passed, and the two lost contact when Daniel went off to college, but Adam was never far from Daniel's memory. As Daniel got older, he felt guilty about the way he had treated the other boy. He knew the chaos of his childhood was partially responsible, but he also knew it could never be an excuse for treating someone that way.

Inspired by his own turbulent past, Daniel decided to major in psychology, in the hopes of helping abused and at-risk children. Despite his unusual skill set, he had no interest in doing work specifically related to blindness. But that was about to change.

One day Daniel was assigned a book in class that completely changed the way he thought about blindness—and his own future. That book, *The Making of Blind Men* by Dr. Robert Scott, offered the audacious thesis that blindness is more a social construct than a disability.

Scott's book spelled out to Daniel what he'd known his whole life: that society, rather than ability, determines what blind people can and cannot do. This was Daniel's aha moment.

In Dr. Scott's view, traditional approaches were preventing blind people from living lives more like Daniel's—a bit riskier, perhaps, but far more fulfilling. It finally dawned on Daniel that Adam had been helpless not by his own design, but by simply following the rules society imposed on blind people.

Daniel realized his knowledge was a gift he needed to share with other blind people, to help them find a new level of freedom. Yet he was about to embark on his master's thesis, on autism and children with neurological conditions. While the subject fascinated him, he now realized it would be just another intellectual exercise, another useless dissertation. Inspired by his new goal—providing other blind people with a path to self-sufficiency—he chose another subject.

"I wanted to do something real," he told me.

He turned to a subject he knew well, but had never really given much intellectual thought to, despite being a sort of pioneer in the field: echolocation. Over the years, Daniel had worked with ten different mobility instructors, whose job was to teach blind people how to move. Not one of them could explain or truly understand what Daniel was doing with the clicks he used to paint a picture of the world around him, most likely because they were all sighted people who couldn't fathom what he was doing because they had no need to use sound in order to "see" like he did. Daniel de-

cided he would try to find a practical application of echolocation for blind people.

This would be his thesis!

Like everything he did, he started the research with
gusto. His advisor, Dr. David Warren, was a perceptual development expert and, it so happened, an authority on blindness. He introduced Daniel to the core body of research on
echolocation.

Under Dr. Warren's direction, Daniel uncovered a surprising amount of literature on the subject—not from mobility experts, but from experimental psychologists or those
in the natural sciences. There was little, if any, application
within the research for the population most affected: those
who are blind.

Daniel changed that.

For his thesis, he managed to do something he'd never
done before: train someone to echolocate. In fact, he taught
twenty-four blind children the technique. When the word got
out, it created a firestorm of both praise and concern, even
hostility—the latter from the blind community itself.

The "leak" to that community about Daniel's research
happened almost by accident. When a presenter at an orientation and mobility convention canceled, Daniel was asked
to fill in. He knew his talk would be controversial, because
the entire industry was predicated on the notion that "blind
people need sighted people to teach blind people how to be
blind," as Daniel puts it.

His study made waves, and soon he was approached by

a university and asked if he would be interested in becoming a mobility specialist. A blind mobility specialist. It had never been done. He had never considered it, but decided to embrace the challenge, entering an orientation and mobility program and getting his second master's degree. Ironically, however, as a blind person, he still couldn't get certified.

But it was Congress that came to the rescue, passing the Americans with Disabilities Act (ADA) in 1990. The new legislation challenged people in hiring positions to justify why they couldn't hire a particular person to do a particular job. Before the ADA, a manager could simply cite an applicant's blindness as the reason. The ADA forced employers to give a justification for turning down the disabled person by listing the various job functions the individual's presumed disability would prevent them from doing.

As Daniel jokes, he wasn't trying to be a bus driver. But there was no reason he couldn't serve competently as an *orientation and mobility specialist* and he soon became certified. "I sort of slipped in while everyone was reeling from this new regulation, and luckily, the university was supportive," he says.

Daniel had righted a long-standing wrong: a blind man could finally help other blind people find their way in the world.

HOW EXACTLY does echolocation work?

Imagine you're in yoga class, meditating with your eyes closed, when you hear a person enter the room. You don't have to guess where the person is, because your ears tell you they are behind you and to your right. You have two ears for a reason: a sound reaches one ear a split second before the other, and your brain takes that information and tells you the direction the sound is coming from; this is called acoustic location.

Echolocation is the reflection of sounds off physical objects back to the animal or person who made those sounds, allowing them to locate those objects. So for instance, when hiking, Daniel can use echolocation to determine that a nearby tree is oddly shaped and that there's a metal fence between him and the tree. He can also tell you, with remarkable precision, how close both the tree and the fence are. Daniel says he has a three-dimensional moving picture of everything around him. It may seem like magic, but, as he insists, it's simply science.

When scientists scanned Daniel's brain, they were surprised to see the part that normally processes visual stimuli—which in blind people tends to atrophy—lit up like a Christmas tree. This is because Daniel's years of practice had retrained the visual center of his brain to process sound the same way it would normally process light. Scientists did not know that this part of the brain could be repurposed in such a dramatic way.

Daniel teaches blind people how to reprogram their brains to see in a nonvisual way by learning how to distinguish between stimuli, and learning which you need to pay attention to and which you don't. The teaching starts with small, hard-surfaced handheld panels. The person learns to sense how close the panels are by making clicking sounds and listening for how the clicks are reflected back to them. Over time, the size and distance of the panels changes, so the student's ability to read the physical objects around them becomes more and more accurate. Eventually, they begin to "see" their environment.

He likens echolocating to playing a piano or speaking a foreign language. It takes some time, but anyone can learn to do it. I asked him how long it took to teach someone echolocation. I assumed it would at least take a few months, if not years, and was surprised when he answered, "It's more on the scale of weeks. In fact, we often start to see differences in just hours."

I was fascinated by Daniel, and had so many other questions for him. But first I had to ask how he rides a bike.

"It requires me to be extremely, *extremely* focused," he said, laughing.

He contrasts his style of cycling with that of sighted people, who generally ride to relax, get exercise, or both. They may have their music playing through headphones while they enjoy the passing scenery.

For Daniel, biking is anything but relaxing. His rides are filled with "lots and lots of clicking, and lots of very, very quick decision-making." He finds a rhythm to it and gets into a trancelike state. That means he can't be riding and chatting with a companion. He has one task: making sure his path is clear.

When mountain biking, a sport that many sighted people don't even try, he generally rides with a sighted person in the lead and a bell on their bike, because single-track trails are often more treacherous than regular roads. He listens to the lead cyclist and their movements, while clicking and feeling the terrain as it changes under his tires.

How about hiking?

"It's like biking, but more relaxed," he says. "You obviously have to pay attention, but it's very much about what your cane is telling you."

Daniel hikes with both a hiking stick and a special long cane. He's constantly aware of where the trail is, and where the trail's *edge* is. And like a mental GPS, he memorizes where he's going and where he's been, so he's not treading new ground on the walk back. Most professional blind hikers still follow a sighted leader, but Daniel and his organization, to his knowledge, are the only ones officially teaching blind people to hike and camp on their own, if they so choose.

NEARLY TWENTY YEARS AGO, Daniel founded the nonprofit World Access for the Blind to allow blind people to direct their own achievements and take control of their lives, as well as to increase public awareness of what blind people are capable of. Near the top of their homepage, they state their goals and methods: "Our Vision Is Sound," "Our Method Is Science," and "Our Results Change Lives." They have helped more than ten thousand people in over forty countries.

Daniel's larger goal is to establish academies where people can be trained to teach these methods in their own countries and regions in a way that's self-empowering. Daniel is insistent that "I don't want to take responsibility for empowering others. That's to be their responsibility."

THE SUBJECT OF NUMEROUS print and television features and interviews, Daniel is a regular speaker and lecturer, and gives a riveting demonstration of echolocation during his TED Talks. His fame has even earned him the nickname "Batman," both for the way he uses echolocation like a bat and the amazing work he's done for others.

His story is an example for everyone, not just those who are blind, of how we can break free of the limits our minds and society have placed on us. "We have all faced barriers, restrictions," Daniel says. "I grew up at a time when it was pretty much unheard of for a blind person to be out on the street on their own, or to own their own property, or to be running their own business, or living without some kind of chaperone. That's changing."

What would Daniel like you to take away from his story?

His message is: "Find and claim your own freedom. I also like to say, share your freedom, because when you have freedom, you have the capacity to give it to others."

TAKE ACTION

WHERE do you feel trapped, held back, or restricted?

_____

_____

_____

_____

_____

WHAT are some ways you can claim your freedom in these areas?

_____

_____

_____

_____

_____

DO what it takes to claim your freedom like Daniel did.

TROY JAMES:
BEND IT LIKE . . .TROY

Troy James walked confidently onto the stage of one of the world's biggest television shows, *America's Got Talent*. Around thirty, he was tall, black, slender but athletic, with a shaved head. He wore a snug-fitting outfit that resembled a tuxedo, until you realized his tie was just printed on his shirt and the whole thing was essentially a unitard plus black shorts. When judge Heidi Klum asked what talent he was going to display, his handsome face lit up with a million-watt smile, and his eyes twinkled with more than a hint of playful devilishness. "You'll see," he replied.

As the judges watched, he first twisted his arms behind him in an improbable reverse self-embrace. With his back to the audience, he began bending backward . . . and bending, and bending, until his hands touched the stage. His pose didn't seem humanly possible . . . but it got weirder.

Now on his hands and feet—but upside down—his body began to quiver and quake as he walked on all fours, resembling some grotesque inverted man-spider. The crowd screamed in horror and glee. He twisted his body as he moved, and the camera found the faces of the judges, wide-eyed with astonishment (and revulsion).

He then descended, crablike, to the judges' platform and confronted them, prompting Simon Cowell to make the sign of the cross with two fingers. Troy climbed back onto the stage and collapsed into a contorted heap, his head torqued to one side, facing the crowd. Then, as if to bring them all back, he flashed that electric smile once again, timed perfectly to the opening chords of Chic's disco-era hit "Le Freak."

It brought the house down.

THIS REAL-LIFE SPIDER-MAN knew very early on he could do things no other kid could do. Troy somehow survived being born an astonishing *five months* premature, and suspects that perhaps some of his connective tissues didn't develop completely. He's still a little afraid to look deeply into it, worried about what he might uncover.

He does know that he has Ehlers-Danlos syndrome (EDS), a group of thirteen disorders that can affect vital bodily systems like the skin, bones, blood vessels, and various organs. Troy has many markers of the syndrome: his arm span is wider than he is tall (and he's tall), and he can bend his fingers back far enough to touch the back of his hand with his fingertips. EDS can deeply hinder most people's ability to do even basic activities—he has heard that some people with EDS have dislocated their legs just getting out of bed. It can also gift (or curse) sufferers with the kind of seemingly insane elasticity—known as hypermobility—that Troy displayed onstage on *America's Got Talent*. While its symptoms can be treated and managed, there is no cure for EDS. But so far, it hasn't held Troy back. Troy has had no pain, and his limbs all seem to go back into place after he's twisted them, so for now, he plans to just enjoy his extraordinary ability. He's counting himself lucky and rolling (or twisting) with it.

AS A KID GROWING UP in Toronto, Canada, Troy's first use for his bendiness was to entertain other kids and have fun. His grandmother found it alarming and told him not to do it, as she feared the Children's Aid Society (Ontario's child protection services) might suspect her or other family members of abusing him and take him away. She even phoned Troy's mother once and implored her, in tears, to get Troy to stop "risking breaking his legs" with his antics. But Troy never got hurt, and his grandmother eventually got used to it.

In elementary school, he was bullied and ostracized for his being so different. But by the time he entered high school, the other kids were mature enough to see Troy not as an object of disdain, but rather as a friend with a pretty cool ability. One even wrote in his yearbook, "Join Cirque du Soleil. Run away and join the circus. It's your destiny." Troy thought it was a nice compliment, but didn't take it too seriously.

Little did he know.

While the notion of a life in the circus sounded fun, Troy dismissed it as a high school fantasy. His practical nature pushed him to enter college. While studying for a degree in occupational health and safety, he took a job at a theme park running a roller coaster to help pay his way through school. His job was to get people loaded into the roller-coaster cars, secure them, hit the start button, wait until they returned, make sure they all got out, rinse, and repeat.

One day, some unexpected maintenance on one of the rides was taking a while, and in the summer heat, the long line of people waiting for the ride grew restless. Troy and his crew knew they might have a full-blown riot on their hands if something didn't happen soon, but Troy had an idea. Despite being a little reluctant to perform for strangers, he began walking up and down the line of park guests, showing them feats of flexibility that they had never seen or dreamed of. The people in that line forgot all about their long wait because this tall young man who could bend like a rubber toy was more entertaining than any roller coaster.

Troy worried that he might be in trouble when his bosses heard of their employee's "show." Instead, they asked if he would be a character in their Halloween Haunt, when the amusement park transformed into a "scary" world of mazes, with monsters roaming the park. "I got to put on the costume with fake blood and chase people in crazy contorted poses and movements, which was so much fun!" he remembers.

And so began Troy James's career as a "creature actor."

HIS HALLOWEEN APPEARANCE led to an offer to reprise his creepy performance in a film, a local Canadian horror production called *The Void*. While his screen time on the finished product was only about five seconds, he had a taste for performing and was interested in doing more. But instead of launching him to stardom, things got quiet after the film. He went on to complete his degree and begin an internship in the HR department at a corporation, the furthest thing from playing twisted and consorted monster characters on camera!

Troy was resigned but also happy to have a steady job. Despite the thrill of entertaining people with his unimaginable talent, he felt it was just plain responsible to have a good, safe job like everyone else. So he let go of his fantasies of working for the circus or in show business.

But just when he thought he had it all figured out . . .

He got an email. Someone he'd worked with on *The Void* a few years earlier wrote to say they were now doing a TV series and wondered if he'd like to be a monster. Troy was excited to take them up on their offer and agreed. It was a major show called *Shadowhunters* for the Freeform network (formerly ABC Family), owned by Disney.

Troy arrived on set and was fitted for his monster suit.

Then he was directed to "creepily crawl toward the main actress on your hands and knees" so he did. They called cut and seemed satisfied. But when they called for the next take, Troy decided to make it interesting. Rather than doing as he'd been directed—and after realizing the producers and director were unaware of his "talents"—he did this take Troy-style, upside down and backward. When someone finally yelled "cut!" the set got very quiet. Like he had at the amusement park, Troy feared he'd done something wrong by horsing around on a serious film set.

The stunned director took him aside. "Troy, can you just . . . uh, I can't direct that," he said, stammering a bit—but clearly delighted. "I'm, uh, not sure what I just saw, but it was freakin' awesome! Can you just do it again—whatever it was—when we roll?"

While Troy was taking everything in on set, one of the creature designers was unknowingly about to change Troy's life. He had shot a 30-second video of Troy "flailing around on the floor" and posted the footage to the internet. It wasn't long before it went viral, garnering millions of views.

"Who or what is this . . . person?" all the comments asked. Talk about blowing up.

"Troy, have you seen this?" his friends texted. "You're all over Facebook! You have to check your social media!"

"Oh my gosh! I couldn't use my phone for twenty-four hours because it was just nonstop notifications," Troy told me. "I woke up to five hundred friend requests!"

The video caught the attention of the producers of *Steve*,

American television host Steve Harvey's talk show, and the next thing Troy knew, he was on his way to New York to appear on the show. It would be his first time on national television—and also his first time traveling out of Canada.

The explosive attention was pretty heady, and quickly overwhelmed him. After all, he was just a guy from Toronto who could bend in crazy ways, so when he was thrust into the limelight, he didn't realize how quickly missing small details could cause a normal situation to snowball into a comedy of errors.

The TV appearances and viral video generated many inquiries, including an excited call from another TV production who thought his video was "amazing" and wanted to book him to perform on their set for two days. Troy happily agreed, but kept two important secrets: he didn't tell the production company he had a regular job, and he didn't tell his regular job about the TV show. That might not have been an issue with any other employer, but Troy happened to work for the HR department of an organization that was a little different from most—but more on that in a moment.

Troy went ahead and booked two "vacation" days to accommodate the production, but being new at this, he didn't take into account the fluidity of entertainment production schedules. He also didn't realize the production company had made another assumption about him.

The day before the shoot, Troy's phone rang at three in the morning. He answered, and it was the production company, frantically asking, "Why are you not here? You were supposed to be here at two!" They also reminded him his makeup would take at least three hours to apply.

Jolted by a rush of adrenaline, Troy leaped out of bed, got dressed, flew out to his car, and hurriedly brushed the snow off it, all while wondering how he'd gotten the shoot date wrong. As he sped to the set, the production kept him on the phone the entire way, demanding moment-to-moment updates: "Where are you now? Okay, now where are you?"

Sick to his stomach with guilt and stress, he just knew that this was going to be his last day as an actor. Arriving at the set, they didn't even let him park his car, instead rushing him to makeup. In the makeup chair, he checked his phone and saw that his worried mother had been calling nonstop as she'd seen him rush out of the house in the early hours of the morning and didn't know why, so he messaged her that he was okay. Then he needed to notify his work that he wouldn't be able to make it, so he began to write a simple "I am unable to come to work today," but someone began applying makeup to his face and someone else took his phone, leaving his message to his coworkers truncated and now slightly ominous: *I am . . .*

After the makeup process, filming began. At one o'clock in the afternoon, they broke for lunch, and Troy finally relaxed a bit. That didn't last long. One of the production team approached him, looking distressed, and said, "Troy, is this a prank? We have a staff sergeant on the phone and he says there's a missing persons report out for you!"

Like I said, Troy didn't work for just some company—
he worked for a government law enforcement department.
The missing persons report had been generated for reasons
including his haunting partial text to his coworkers and an
accident on the highway Troy usually took on his commute.

Oh yeah, and the seventy voicemails and text messages
sent to him without a response.

As Troy wondered how on earth they'd found him, since
he'd told no one where he was going, it dawned on him:
"They're police. They're detectives. Finding missing people
is what they do."

Once that mystery had been cleared up and Troy had
explained to both sides what had happened, the cast and
crew wondered how he'd gotten the dates wrong. As Troy
fumbled for an answer, an experienced actor asked the winning question: "Troy, why didn't your agent tell you your
shoot was today?"

Troy looked blank. "What's an agent?"

The actor introduced Troy to his own agent, and Troy
signed with him right away to avoid further mishaps. Sometimes what you don't know can hurt you. Having learned a
very important lesson about life in show business, a chas-
tened Troy went back to the office and threw himself into
being the best HR person ever. He resolved to never let them
down again and to grow old in the job. He saw himself as
a productive adult. "I had a real job at an office with a desk
and a name tag," he told me. It felt safe.

That lasted about two months.

After the video and media interest, Troy had been getting various production offers (including some from circuses), but turned most of them down. And yet they kept coming, some from as far off as Japan. He knew he had to make a change soon. But he feared leaving the stable ship of office life for what might be the stormy high seas of show biz.

But he felt the draw powerfully, and quite frankly, he loved it.

When he finally made the decision to leave and told his coworkers, they were tremendously supportive, and still are, a few years later. Yes, there are no guarantees in the entertainment industry, but expressing himself as an artist was too important to Troy. His appearance on *America's Got Talent* gave his career a huge boost, and he's gone on to work on films like 2019's *Hellboy* and hit TV shows including *The Flash* and *The Strain*.

He's also had wonderful travel opportunities that have taken him to New York, Japan, Spain, Portugal, Germany, and even Cape Town, South Africa. But the best was yet to come. As exciting as all the travel and television and film jobs have been, Troy was beside himself with excitement when he was invited to compete for the prestigious prize at the 2019 Festival Mondial du Cirque de Demain ("World Festival of the Circus of Tomorrow") in Paris. Open to a variety of circus-style performers including clowns, tightrope walkers, acrobats, jugglers, and trapeze artists, the festival also allows contortionists to compete. It's considered the Olympics of the circus arts.

Too flustered to take on the performing task by himself, Troy recruited one of his bendy buddies, Ess Hödlmoser, to create a show with him.

The contestants at Cirque de Demaine are the best in the world, and although Troy and Ess did not win the coveted prize, they were honored to take part.

SO, HOW HAS IT WORKED OUT, leaving security to follow his passion?

"I was happy before, but I'm even happier now," Troy says. "It's just gotten better and better. I'm constantly in shock every time something new happens and I get to meet new people and fly to a new place. And everyone is so nice."

Not surprising, now that I know Troy James. Who could not be nice to such a sweet, humble man? Troy knows now that success can come in many forms, not just a secure office job.

It's a delight to watch Troy perform for people—not just for the inconceivable ways in which he contorts his body, but for the huge joy he obviously gets from people's reactions. He is so quick to give you that sunny smile, and you can tell the man behind it is just as warm and open.

I asked him what message he wanted you to take away from his story.

"I'm living proof that you can and should follow your dreams," he says. "My friends in high school saw something years before I did when they wrote 'join the circus' in my yearbook. I feel like a fraud saying this, because I'm totally a shy person, but don't be shy. Because you never know who's watching. Someone saw me and took a chance on me."

Troy says if you like to dance, dance. If you like singing, then sing. "If I had not taken this leap of faith because I was worried what people would think, I'd still be behind the desk right now. Go out there and do it. Show someone, because you never know where that will take you."

Despite his youth, Troy is well aware that we're only here for a short time. "I think we should try to maximize our happiness and to do what we love. I know it's easier said than done, but take the time to really explore what your passion is and see how you can incorporate that in your life. I had a path chosen, but something better came along. Find your passion, follow it, work for it, and own it, because it's the real you."

TAKE ACTION

WHAT IS SOMETHING you've always wanted to do or dreamed of doing? Painting, singing, dance, learning a language, learning to code, travel?

_____

_____

_____

_____

_____

_____

_____

Now do it! You can find salsa classes on Groupon and affordable language classes on Audible. Buy art supplies and start creating, or join a local choir. No matter your budget or current skill level, make the time to start doing more of the things that bring you joy, the things you are passionate about. Follow your bliss, alongside your current career for now, and see where it takes you. Then when you feel ready to make the switch, take the leap of faith.

KYLE MAYNARD:
NO EXCUSES

Every foot—every inch—was a grinding, miserable test of will. The unforgiving cold, the gnawing gusts of painfully thin air, the loose rocks that either gave way under him or threatened to rain down upon him at every turn, were taking their toll on his body, spirit, and soul.

Ascending brutal 40-degree slopes, climbing three feet then slipping back four, Kyle Maynard somehow found the strength to persevere. He just kept climbing, focusing on the *single foot* of mountain in front him. But there were moments—many of them—when all he wanted to do was call it quits and go back down.

But he couldn't, because this wasn't just about getting to the top of Africa's tallest mountain, Kilimanjaro. It was a sacred pact he'd made with himself.

He would not quit, and he would not fail, for this was no ordinary climb and he was no ordinary climber.

Kyle Maynard is a quadruple amputee. Born with partial arms and legs, his arms end at the elbow, his legs at the knee.

Forgoing any prosthetics, but fitted with special accommodations like rubber caps on the ends of his short limbs and aids against the cold—even chains to help with traction—he was essentially bear crawling to the Roof of Africa.

Kyle Maynard's mission was a tribute to extraordinary bravery. Around his neck was something so precious that he struggled those last few hundred yards to ensure it reached the summit, no matter the cost.

SIX YEARS EARLIER, a chance encounter at an airport had set Kyle on a powerful new trajectory. Even at that point, he was staggeringly accomplished for a young man with no limbs, but there was still room in his heart to push himself further.

That day, two members of the military police approached Kyle as he waited for a plane and stopped to tell him their story. They had both been horribly burned in an ambush in Iraq. In their darkest moment, lying side by side in the hospital, they contemplated giving up on life to escape the agonizing dead end they felt awaited them. But later that day, fate intervened. They happened to see an inspiring story on television about a remarkable man . . . Kyle Maynard.

Kyle's bravery renewed their faith, and they committed to a pact: they would press on, conquer their adversity, and somehow piece together their shattered lives.

When Kyle heard this, it changed his life. He maintained his composure with the soldiers, but as soon as he got back to his hotel, he broke down. "I cried for hours," he told me. Even now, he admits, "I think about those guys almost every day."

Six years later, he began his epic climb in Africa. The precious cargo around his neck was a vial filled with the ashes of a fallen soldier. Kyle's unbelievable expedition was to commemorate the bravery of that fallen soldier and to honor all fallen heroes.

KYLE CAME INTO THIS WORLD with what is called congenital amputation, a condition where a baby is born without full limbs. The exact cause is not known, but various theories exist, from fibrous amniotic bands that entangle the limbs and reduce or cut off blood flow to radiation, certain drugs, chemicals, even in-utero infections. The moment of his birth was quite a shock for his parents, Scott and Anita Maynard. As his mother puts it, "When he was born, the doctors covered him in a towel and whisked him away before we could see him."

Congenital amputation usually affects one or two limbs, but almost never all four. In that respect, Kyle was quite rare. "All we knew was that he was a beautiful baby. He was glowing. We just focused on that gorgeous face," his mother said. His lack of arms or legs couldn't begin to dim their love for Kyle.

KYLE WAS BORN in Washington, DC, but his parents soon moved to Indiana, where he grew up. Kyle was fed and cared for like any other infant; when he reached toddlerhood, his mother felt they should continue to feed him, but his father put his foot down, fearing this would set a precedent for reliance on others that couldn't be undone as Kyle got older. Scott, a former military man, felt strongly that Kyle needed to grow up to be self-sufficient and never rely solely on others. So from early on, his parents resolved to treat him "as normally as possible," allowing him to fail and even take a few bumps in the process. They would give him all the love they had, but no special treatment.

Having retrained as an engineer after leaving the military, Scott handcrafted everything from spoons to tricycles to bikes to accommodate his son's condition. But as Kyle grew older, his parents realized that they had something bigger to worry about than protecting him: trying to hold him back.

Friends came easily to Kyle; he was gregarious, always the center of activity. His childhood was idyllic, and despite his physical disadvantages, all the kids in the neighborhood and at school accepted him.

Around three or four, he began to understand that he was different, but since his family treated him normally, he didn't feel any stigma or shame. Kyle's grandmother, like his mother, had the impulse to shield him from disappointment and harm, but she also taught him to hold his head up high in public and to greet people. This friendly, confident tactic helped uncertain bystanders drop their guards and warm to him.

As a young boy, Kyle was always thinking about what he would be when he grew up. With a former soldier as a dad, it was no surprise that he saw himself as a man of ac-

IONE BUTLER

tion, perhaps an Army Ranger, jumping out of planes and going after bad guys, defending the defenseless. Years later, in high school, he even tried to join the military. Looking him over, the recruiter suggested he could be a chaplain.

"Okay, that's cool. Does the chaplain get a gun?" Kyle asked.

"Chaplain? Gun? Uh, no," the recruiter replied. And that was the end of that.

When he was ten, now with three little sisters to keep him company, Kyle's family moved to Georgia. Gone suddenly were his close circle of friends and the sympathetic community who saw him as a regular boy. He was surrounded by strangers, and the glares and taunts and cruelty were soul-crushing, even for a tough little kid with big dreams. On top of that, his parents were having financial and marital issues that ratcheted up the tension at home. Kyle had never felt so low.

After getting sick at school one day, he went home to recuperate and turned on a pro basketball game. Already depressed, he felt even more thoroughly defeated as he watched the game, knowing he'd never be able to play like that. Bereft of hope, this was the last straw. The pressures had become too much, and he was ready to end it all. He got out a belt and tried to hang himself from his bunk bed, but he "couldn't even do that," he confessed.

SHORTLY AFTER his failed suicide attempt he resigned to live life as best he could. He soon made it through that emotional rough patch and began his fight for acceptance in a new group of friends. In sixth grade, Kyle expressed an interest in football, but was adamant that he would not be the water boy, a position they'd normally give to kids with disabilities. While Anita had always been more protective of her son than Scott, she surprised everyone by phoning the coach to lobby for a position for Kyle on the squad.

The coach agreed with Anita that Kyle deserved a real shot, so, in spite of not having limbs, Kyle was given the job of nose tackle, the football equivalent of a brick wall. What he lacked in mobility, he more than made up for in ferocity and sheer grit, and quickly developed a reputation as a formidable adversary. His technique was to ram his helmet into the shins of the opposing players, and for a while, it worked.

But soon his parents realized that their son needed a sport where his lack of mass would be less of a disadvantage, a sport that was literally based on weight—like wrestling. A former wrestler himself, Scott proposed Kyle try the sport, and Kyle agreed, plunging in. But it proved to be a different story than football.

He lost all thirty-five of his matches over his first two years of wrestling.

It was immensely discouraging, but Scott wouldn't let Kyle feel sorry for himself. Like Kyle's own personal life coach, his dad encouraged him, sometimes pushed him hard, and never let him wallow.

It was also during this time that Kyle was beginning to

discover the writings of great thinkers and also read stories about people who had been summarily defeated in nearly countless efforts, but went on to astonishing successes. These days, Kyle is a font of philosophical knowledge, frequently quoting the wisdom of great minds from Buddha to Solzhenitsyn to Joseph Campbell. But back then, just getting his feet wet in the inspirations of the greats, he reasoned that those thirty-five losses were merely thirty-five opportunities to develop his skills, thirty-five no's closer to yes. He was beginning to understand the power of failure.

He kept on. Guided and pushed by his dad, along with his wrestling coach and mentor, Cliff Ramos, Kyle took on a grueling weight-training program to build his body into a slab of pure muscle. Kyle would become so strong, in terms of his power-to-weight ratio, that his opponents would complain about his "unfair advantage"—despite the irony of these complaints hiding in plain sight. With Cliff's seasoned advice, Kyle also used his mind to develop specific attacks on his opponents—strategies designed specifically for a man with no arms and legs.

It finally worked, and in his senior year, he began chalking up one win after another. People would come from far and wide to see "the kid with no arms and legs" wrestle, and they would go wild when he won, which now seemed to happen every time he climbed onto the mat.

When TV crews and reporters showed up in droves to interview him, his teammates sometimes grumbled about Kyle getting all the attention. They pointed out that there were better wrestlers on the squad, some even headed to illustrious colleges on wrestling scholarships. Sometimes they even wondered aloud why the press was so interested in Kyle. They, like his childhood playmates in Indiana, had grown so used to Kyle the friend and competitor that they had completely forgotten his disability.

Kyle would go on to accumulate an astounding thirty-six victories, even qualifying for the Georgia state wrestling championship—none of which would have been possible were it not for those first thirty-five losses.

THE IDEA OF A KID without arms and legs becoming a high school wrestler—let alone a champion high school wrestler—seemed more than worthy of a book. So at eighteen, Kyle wrote *No Excuses: The True Story of a Congenital Amputee Who Became a Champion in Wrestling and in Life*. And if you're wondering whether he dictated it, think again: Kyle can type 50 words per minute.

Kyle wanted to use his book to motivate people to draw strength from him and rise to overcome their own life challenges, no matter what they were. The book has become an inspiration for many, including those who wrote the rave reviews found on the first page, superstars like Troy Aikman, Wayne Gretzky, and Arnold Schwarzenegger. He was invited to speak at an event for wrestling players and coaches. It was so successful he soon began speaking professionally. For help with his first paid speech, he turned to one of his biggest fans: his beloved grandmother. The speech was an instant hit, and he has never looked back.

Kyle is very engaging, a supremely polite and motivated conversationalist, but there's also a fire in his eyes, a rare intensity of spirit that no doubt fuels everything he does. As someone who has done so much to help others, one of his favorite lines might seem counterintuitive at first: "'Anything is possible' is a lie," he says. "By knowing our limits, we know what we have to test in ourselves. Without that, it's an assumption. Know your limits—but never stop trying to break them."

To highlight his point, Kyle explains, "I can't bench ten thousand pounds, no matter how much I try. But I can improve what I can bench. It's the same with anything else; any limit can be tested." Kyle may not be able to lift ten thousand pounds, but in 2004 he received GNC's World's Strongest Teen award when he bench-pressed a staggering 240 pounds—twenty-three times!

SO, HAVING CONQUERED WRESTLING, writing, motivational speaking, and Kilimanjaro, what was left for this extraordinary man?

Climbing another mountain.

In 2016 Kyle faced down a new opponent: Argentina's Mount Aconcagua. Aconcagua, with its massive western flanks spreading into neighboring Chile, is a tougher climb than Kilimanjaro. At 22,841 feet, it's the tallest mountain outside of Asia. It's remote, it's steep, and it's really cold. The Federal Aviation Administration (FAA) requires that all pilots in unpressurized aircraft use supplemental oxygen above 14,000 feet—and Aconcagua's summit is nearly *9,000 feet higher*. Yes, Everest climbers go higher still, but they also spend very little time at that altitude. Kyle did not have that luxury. The average climber takes around a week to summit Aconcagua; it took Kyle more like a month. At the top, the air pressure is only 40 percent of what it is at sea level, and the oxygen level is halved.

Why on earth would Kyle attempt such a daring climb?

"My purpose in life is to show other people their purpose," he explains. "Help show them their true capabilities, their human potential." What better way to do that than by going out and doing the impossible?

While he'd learned some of the ropes of high-altitude climbing on Kilimanjaro, Aconcagua was "the hardest physical test I've ever had, but also the most beautiful view I've ever had," Kyle says.

Once he began climbing—or more accurately, bear crawling—Kyle realized Aconcagua wasn't going to be a 22,000-foot climb. It was going to be a *three-foot climb*.

Since Kilimanjaro, Kyle had broadened his horizon from one foot to three. "I would take a breath and do three feet. Take a breath and get another three feet. A breath and three more. I'd just think about all I can see right now. It's three feet."

His pain on Kilimanjaro had been intense. On Aconcagua, the pain he expereinced dragging himself up the mountain was exquisite, a whole new level of unbearable. As he approached the summit, his body began to shut down from hypothermia. The cold was so daunting that he feared he wouldn't make it. He was shivering uncontrollably. At one point, as he stopped to rest, he looked over and saw a spot a few yards away where a fellow American had died just the day before.

Aconcagua is nicknamed the "Mountain of Death," and its grim epithet is well earned. Even in the summer, temperatures on its slopes can fall well below −20°F. On top of that, the low oxygen robs the body of the ability to keep itself warm, which adds to the climber's vulnerability. The peak's nickname comes mostly from the many who have lost their lives due to extreme loss of body heat during the climb.

Despite this, Kyle defeated Aconcagua, and saw his success as a victory for so many others. He battled his way to the summit using every iota of tenacity he had, just as he had when overcoming every other obstacle in his life. Kyle explains that when confronted with a problem, whether it's three feet or three hours or three anything, "I'll do my best for those three, then I'll get another three, and another three, and keep at it until I get to the top or end of whatever it is."

BEING AROUND KYLE is always an uplifting experience. I had an opportunity to spend some time with him after a chance encounter at Burning Man, the annual cultural and community event held in Nevada's Black Rock Desert. It was many months after I had interviewed him for this book, and we bumped into each other at the end of a beautiful Sunday service. He asked if he could ride back to LA with me when the festival ended the next day. Since there is no phone service in the area, I told him to meet me at my camp by eight p.m., as I would be heading out with friends to watch the temple burn, a Burning Man tradition. As I cycled off, I wondered how on earth this man with no limbs would be able to make his way the five miles to my camp with all his stuff. Of course, I should have known better. He showed up at seven fifteen on a custom-made bike, his belongings tied to the back.

Even the bike had a story. Kyle had it built to retrace the trek of the Spartan king Leonidas and his army, those three hundred warriors who faced more than one hundred thousand Persians in the epic Battle of Thermopylae. Kyle, more than most, appreciates the underdog grit of the Spartans. He did the trek to raise funds and awareness for the Navy SEAL Foundation.

Kyle continued to impress me with his resourcefulness and ability to just get on with things. I asked him if he'd ever considered prosthetics. "I tried them once, but they slowed me down," he said.

That answer didn't really surprise me. Kyle was also pretty outspoken about the way society sees disability. Like Daniel Kish, Kyle feels that the way people are taught to help those with disabilities is not often what they actually need. To underscore this sentiment, he told me about a gate agent at an airport who wanted to push him in his wheelchair to his next gate. When he told her he'd been sitting on a plane for a while and preferred to do it himself, she actually got angry with him for being "ungrateful" for her help. "If we don't let people go through some of those struggles on their own," he says, "and deal with things and learn how to cope, learn how to use your mind, not fall apart when something bad happens to you, then it sets you up for a bigger fall later on."

On our way back to Los Angeles, we stopped for a night in Reno. My friends were impressed by Kyle, commenting on how easily he got himself around the casino, climbing up on stools at the gaming tables, holding his cards, and gambling like everyone else. Nothing stops this man, and yet he admits it used to bother him to be seen as an inspiration. For Kyle, getting recognition and praise for doing "normal things" made him feel too different. However, he told me, after his recent experience at Burning Man, surrounded by radical love, openness, and expression, his views had shifted. He finally accepted that he is different, and that his way of navigating the world, figuring things out, and not making excuses *is* inspiring to others, which is of course what keeps him going. Kyle is a testament to what you can achieve when you constantly push your limits. And now that he's gotten to the top of two of Earth's highest patches of real estate, what message would Kyle like you to take away from his story?

"Find your mountain. Find your why. Find your truth."

I cannot wait to see what he has in store next.

TAKE ACTION

1. What is something you once thought was impossible, something that you struggled with and were not sure you could do, but managed to figure out? This could be something as big as getting through college or starting a business, or as small as installing some window blinds (something I was very proud of myself for doing recently).

_____

_____

_____

_____

_____

_____

_____

_____

2. What did you do to accomplish this seemingly impossible or difficult task?

_____

_____

_____

_____

_____

_____

_____

3. Acknowledge this and other times that you have pushed through, persevered, and accomplished something. It's essential to acknowledge and recognize these wins, no matter how big or small, to remind yourself what you are capable of.

AFTERWORD

The motivation for creating *Uplifting Content*—the website, podcast, and this book—came from the discovery that positive stories helped improve my mood, and so it became my mission to deliver this healing idea to as many people as I could.

While I wanted this book to be entertaining, it is primarily a collection of positive anecdotes presenting situations and specific points of view to help anyone dealing with a challenge or, at the very least, to lift your spirits. As I've mentioned, these stories are not intended to be read just once, necessarily—I hope you pick this book back up again and again and use it as a tool for inspiration, relief, and hope whenever you need it.

We humans have been creating and retelling myths for millennia as a way of explaining our sometimes inexplicable world and passing lessons down through generations. We tell stories to lift ourselves and others

So it is with this book.

In the fall of 2019, I interviewed two guests for *The Uplifting Content Podcast* who both spoke a lot about how the stories we tell ourselves have a big impact in our lives. Hearing this in consecutive interviews from guests with completely different backgrounds, I felt as if an outside force was insisting I pay attention to the concept.

The first of these guests, Flip Flippen, is an entrepreneur, philanthropist, and author of many books, including *Your Third Story: Author the Life You Were Meant to Live*. During our interview, Flip spoke about the three different types of stories of our lives. The first, the one we don't have much control over, is the story of where we were born, who our family is, the school we went to, what we were taught, what happened in our childhood, etc. While we did get to make some choices in our childhood, we did not author that first story because it was written for us by the adults that had control over our lives. For some people, this story defines the rest of their lives.

The second story starts in adolescence, Flip explained. That's the time we start telling ourselves things that are often not true, things like I'm not good enough, attractive enough, or smart enough, no one cares about me, I'm boring etc. What were some of the things you told yourself in your adolescence? Were those things true, and how did those beliefs impact you? Flip explained that the tragedy is, some people never stop telling themselves these mistruths and continue to believe them for the rest of their lives.

The third story is the one you get to author. By reframing what has happened to you in the past, changing the narrative, and writing your life story, you get to take back control of it.

The second guest was Lori Gottlieb, a psychotherapist

and author of *The Atlantic*'s "Dear Therapist" column and the book *Maybe You Should Talk to Someone*. She explained that she works with patients with an editor's mind-set, asking questions like, "Is the protagonist moving forward or are they going in circles? Do the plot points reveal a theme?"

Spoiler alert: They always do.

She also asks if the supporting characters (friends, family, coworkers) are important, or are they a distraction? Then Lori works with her patients to examine the stories they've been telling themselves—but this time from the perspective of others—to find the places where the two stories overlap and where there are differences. She then helps her patients write a new narrative that better serves them.

Why have I been going on so much about stories? Because they shape what we think about ourselves, others, and the world around us. Our thoughts and beliefs affect our actions, which, in turn, shape our reality. By making a conscious choice to cut out salacious, divisive, fearmongering, and hateful media and replace it with more positive, inspiring content—like this book—you'll find you have fewer thoughts of worry, less fear, and less anger. My goal for this book is that reading it makes you feel better, lighter, and more motivated to pursue the things you're passionate about, and hopefully, that you then start seeing improvements in your life.

I want to leave you with one last exercise from life coach Noelle Cordeaux, which is an instant pick-me-up: Write, in long form, the story of your life as you want it to be five to ten years from now, writing as if it has already happened and everything has gone as well as it possibly could and you accomplished all the things you wanted to do. Give it a go—have fun with it, notice how it makes you feel, and pay attention to what you write. It will be a clue as to what you really want and what really matters to you in your life.

Come back to this book when you're feeling low or in need of inspiration and hope. Share your successes and how you got on with the exercises with me on social media @ionebutler. Part of the story I've written for my life is that this book does well and becomes the first in a series of Uplifting Stories books, so stay tuned—you'll know I practice what I preach when the next one comes out!

Much love,
Ione

ACKNOWLEDGMENTS

To my friends and family, thank you for all your love and support, it's what keeps me moving forward.

To Prince Ea, thank you for your wisdom and guidance as I began this endeavor. To Adam Siddiq, thank you for planting the seed and inspiring me to create this book. To Chris Voss, thank you for introducing me to Steve. To my agent, Steve Ross, thank you for seeing the potential and believing in *Uplifting Stories* right off the bat, securing a book deal, and for your patience with me!

To my manager, Daniel Pancotto, thank you for supporting my journey as a writer and actress.

Thank you to everyone at Tiller Press/Simon & Schuster for your talent and efforts in getting this out to the world, especially Emily Carleton.

Thank you to everyone I interviewed for the book (even those whose stories I wasn't able to include), for taking the time to share your story and for being the light you are in the world.

To my team, John, Roanne, and Karen, thank you for helping bring all of this together.

ACKNOWLEDGMENTS

To the *Uplifting Content* audience, anyone who shares our posts or listens to the podcast, and to you, the reader of this book, I do this for you, so thank you.

Lastly, to Matt Hansen, thank you. Without your talent, this book wouldn't be as beautiful and moving as it needed to be.